REAL MEN WORSHIP

Real Men Worship

■ ■ ■ ■ ■

LaMar Boschman

VINE
BOOKS
Servant Publications
Ann Arbor, Michigan

Vine Books is an imprint of Servant Publications especially designed to serve evangelical Christians.

Although the stories in this book are true, names and identifying details have been changed to protect the privacy of those involved.

Published by Servant Publications
P.O. Box 8617
Ann Arbor, Michigan 48107

Cover design: Eric Walljasper

97 98 99 00   10 9 8 7 6 5 4 3 2

Printed in the United States of America
ISBN 0-89283-936-8

LIBRARY OF CONGRESS CATALOGING-IN-PUBLICATION DATA

Boschman, LaMar.
    Real men worship / LaMar Boschman.
        p.   cm.
    Includes bibliographical references.
    ISBN 0-89283-936-8
    1. Men—Religious life.   2. Worship.   I. Title.
BV4528.2.B67   1996
248.8'42—dc20   96-32166
                                                                    CIP

Contents

Introduction

I GAVE MY LIFE TO CHRIST when I was only ten. It was the mid-sixties, and that summer my parents moved from central Washington to Prince George, British Columbia in search of a better living. My father, a farmer, was a Mennonite; in fact, he was named after Menno Simmons, the founder of the Mennonites. All Boschmans were Dutch Mennonites—frugal, traditional, and conservative.

Our Mennonite lifestyle was more than a denominational preference; it was a culture. The men were strong and strict, the lords of their homes. Elders were addressed as "sir," even if they were only slightly older. In our worship services it was tradition for the men to sit on one side of the church, women on the other. The men sang bass; the melody and higher parts were for women. Some Mennonites worshiped by singing only the melody because harmony is not mentioned in the Bible. Harmony, as well as rhythm, was thought by some to be worldly and possibly lustful. Others thought that using any musical instruments in worship was wrong. No Mennonite man ever said "Amen" in a service or lifted his hands to worship. To be expressive in any way would certainly be unmanly.

But my father loved music, and he would sit on our porch or in the living room playing his guitar and singing popular country-western or gospel music. He showed me a few chords, and before long I was hooked. For my fourteenth birthday, my parents presented me with the birthday present that would set the course of my life—an acoustic guitar of my very own.

During that year, I spent many hours learning new chords and writing my own songs. At fifteen, a friend and I won a talent contest at our high school singing "Folsom Prison Blues." Encouraged with visions of stardom, I kept working at it until, at sixteen, I recorded my first album with a group called the Goldenaires. The album was a collection of country and gospel tunes, some of which I had written.

When I finished high school, I decided that if I was going to "make it" in the Christian music world I would have to move to the biggest city in British Columbia. At eighteen, I left home bound for Vancouver to look for fame and fortune. I eventually recorded another album with a group known as the Lapels. We had reasonable success singing in churches and concerts regionally, and the album we recorded received air time on both Christian and secular stations in Washington and British Columbia.

One day the drummer and leader of the group suggested that we go to a nondenominational church noted for its great music on Sunday nights. *Why not?* I thought. The Mennonite churches I had visited in Vancouver seemed dry and unfriendly, with piano and organ music that didn't exactly move me. I decided to give it a try.

People told us we would have to arrive at the church early to get a seat for the evening service, so we did. Nine hundred people packed the building. They were listening to the band tune their instruments while waiting for the service to begin. Down the hall I could hear the loud voices of people chanting in prayer. This was certainly different than anything I was used to.

At precisely seven o'clock the ushers cleared the aisles. The choir came marching down the center two aisles toward the front platform, singing in four-part harmony, their purple robes flowing behind them. The hair on my neck stood up. I felt weak all over. This choir had a power and a spirit I had never experienced.

They filled the front of the sanctuary, one hundred twenty of them. I was impressed by the number of men who sang tenor and bass. The organ and piano were lively; the drums and brass were loud. They even had a guitar and a string section. I was in gospel music heaven.

They were singing some of the same songs our group sang. But there was something different about the way they performed them. There was a power in their music that I wanted desperately. After that evening, I attended the church often to find out what made this "on-fire choir" so unique. Later I realized it was the power of the Holy Spirit in their music. They would pray for one hour before each service asking God to use the music to touch people. I became their greatest fan.

I was not used to many "Amens" and "praise the Lords" in the middle of a worship service. But during one of those services I felt the Lord impress on my heart the Scripture verse in Psalms 134:2: "Lift your hands in the sanctuary, bless the Lord" (NKJV). I wrestled internally with what that scripture meant.

Lord, lifting hands is for the Pentecostals, I argued. *They need that emotional release.*

Then I felt the Lord's instruction in my spirit even more strongly: "Lift your hands and bless the Lord."

Father, I'm a Mennonite. We don't lift our hands, I explained to God, expecting some exemption from the command of this scripture because of my denominational background.

But the Lord would not leave me alone. The next time He was even more firm. "Lift your hands in the sanctuary, and bless the Lord!"

I was stuck. I loved the Lord, and I knew I would have to obey Him. I will never forget how hard it was to lift my hands. I was afraid everyone would look at me, but I knew I had to do it. So I lifted my right hand behind the head of the man in front of me and looked around to see if anyone noticed. No one seemed interested. So I raised my hand higher.

What a sensation! I felt light, as if in flight. My spirit was elated as I raised my hands high over my head. I felt free and joy-filled. Suddenly I wanted everyone to see me with my hands in the air. But no one was watching me, for they had their eyes closed and were singing to God. That day I took a major step toward expressing myself in worship publicly. And it would get better still.

I have had to overcome many obstacles on my journey to wholehearted worship. Foremost, I have had to give up my desire to be a star performer instead of a worshiper, and I have had to forsake my false notions about what it means for a man to worship as I learned it in a traditional, quiet, and conservative denomination. Given my stoic Dutch background, I wonder how I could have ever become a wholehearted, expressive worshiper. I had to sort through a lot of religious tradition before I really became "free," but God was leading me in ways He wanted me to grow.

Is there anything about your worship that sets you apart from someone who is worshiping right beside you that does not know the Lord? Is there something standing in your way from wholehearted worship of the Lord? Perhaps you were saved when you were young, and now you are older, married with children, and respected in the community. But as you've grown, your worship life has not grown with you. Or you have learned from your upbringing to worship in the conservative way, without much expression, and have not grown beyond that tradition. No doubt the last ten or twenty years may have brought you through challenging situations and encounters. Maybe the cares of this world have slowed your spiritual momentum and have hindered your worship. Perhaps you are discouraged. For whatever reason, if you are not now able—or if you have never been able—to worship God freely, without reservation and with wholehearted expressiveness, I have good news for you. God wants to renew your worship!

"I tell you the truth," Jesus said. "Anyone who will not receive the kingdom of God like a little child will never enter it" (Lk 18:17, NIV). Perhaps we need to become more like a child in our worship. Perhaps we need to lay aside our burdens, fears, and learned methods of worship. We need to abandon ourselves to the Lord.

It is a difficult thing to become free in worship. But wholehearted worship is a significant part of what being a real man is all about. If we are to be followers of Jesus Christ—*The* Real Man—we must take a look at ourselves and how we are fulfilling the roles God has ordained for us. It not only takes renewing the way we look at worship, but it may also mean adjusting many aspects of our lives. Just as we have to become meek before we know real strength, we may need to become as a little child in order to worship as a man. This kind of growth takes guts, boldness, and a passion for the Lord, but this is exactly what real manhood is all about.

■ ■ ■ ■ ■

ONE

Manhood: A Lost Art?

I have just begun to learn how to "surf the Internet." All the new terms and procedures were terribly confusing at first. My first experience came after I received several offers from America Online. They allowed their new customers to try their program for ten hours free. I was too busy to try it more than once. Months later I received another promotion offering another ten hours free. So I gave them my credit card number and logged in again.

I didn't realize that I now had *two* accounts. Each time I had used a different password. I hadn't written down the first password anywhere because I thought I would remember it. But now I couldn't remember and I couldn't open up the program. I used all the names and numbers that I normally use for passwords or PIN numbers. Nothing worked.

I called the company and went through an endless series of recorded messages and procedures for getting around the basic problem: I had forgotten the password— the key that made everything else work. Finally, I had to go back and start all over with a new account.

Like logging onto the Internet, there are some things in life that can never be figured out unless we start with the correct code. Then it all becomes very simple. Manhood is one of them. Trying to define or understand manhood without God's perspective is like hacking for a password using an infinite number of variables. God's Word gives us the key, and if we lose it, we're in big trouble.

SEARCHING FOR TRUTH
IN THE TWILIGHT ZONE

So often people reject the really simple answer to a problem and begin to look for increasingly complex ones. When we reject the truth, we embark on a journey to a strange sort of Twilight Zone, something akin to Alice's Wonderland, where simplicity is replaced with bizarre perceptions of reality.

Take Harry, for example (not his real name). Harry was the stereotypical cop—Caucasian, six-feet-two-inches tall with a very muscular build. He was tough on the outside and knew all about life on the streets. Harry knew how the drug pipeline worked, and he could get whatever he wanted, anytime he wanted. Feeling above the law, because he *was* the law, he had told me how a person could get out of traffic tickets or lie his way out of all kinds of situations. Harry was "bad" and proud of it.

After Harry gave his life to the Lord, he had a new passion to know God. But the old life didn't totally go away. He didn't cut out the root and die to the passions of his "old man." On Sunday morning he could worship like the rest of us. With hands raised, eyes closed, face toward heaven and tears rolling down the cheeks, Harry would cry out to God. Yet he was still beating his wife and making deals with criminals.

Harry told me many times he wanted to change. He even went through counseling. But he was always looking for a quick fix or an easy answer that circumvented the real issue in his life. I didn't know it at the time, but he was buying, selling, and taking drugs while he was receiving counseling.

The Christian counselor listened patiently to Harry's frustrations and the disagreements between him and his wife. Harry responded to every suggestion with, "I've tried that," or, "I know that." Eventually, they would come back around to the simplest answer of all—repent and stop it! But Harry continued to reject the truth.

It is hard to stop "cold turkey" those habits that are firmly rooted in our lives. But Harry and his wife avoided the obvious and necessary answer to their problems. The truth evaded them over the many years they went through counseling. Eventually, they moved from state to state to stay ahead of their creditors because they didn't want to change their lifestyle.

Harry and his wife lost their way in life. In the end, they destroyed their marriage and lost the respect of their children. Finally, Harry wound up in prison.

Harry refused to accept God's simple truth of repentance. When we refuse to accept God's way, it is as if we are cut loose from an anchor and we begin to float adrift in a sea of bizarre perception of right and wrong, truth and falsehood. We are searching for answers in the Twilight Zone, but never come to a knowledge of the truth.

BREAKING THE CODE

During World War II, Allied Intelligence was able to break the ciphered codes of both the Germans and the Japanese. Intercepted messages looked like lines of random letters that made no sense—that is, until the key element of the code was broken. Then what looked like unintelligible gibberish was quickly transformed into the secret messages of the enemy. Breaking the code was, perhaps, one of the main reasons that, in both the European and Pacific theaters, the Allies were successful.

This principle can be transferred to our own lives. When we reject God's revealed truth, it is like losing the key element of the code to life. As a result, our meaning, purpose, and reality become confused and distorted. Today there are many strange ideas—unintelligible gibberish—about manhood because many men have rejected the self-evident truth revealed by God through nature and in His Word. We have become victims of our own foolish speculations.

Romans chapter one has a lot to say about why and from where people get strange ideas. Romans 1:18-23 says:

The wrath of God is being revealed from heaven against all the godlessness and wickedness of men who *suppress the truth* by their wickedness, since what may be known about God is plain to them, because *God has made it plain* to them. For since the creation of the world God's invisible qualities—his eternal power and divine nature—have been clearly seen, being understood from what has been made, so that men are without excuse.

For although they knew God, they neither glorified him as God nor gave thanks to him, but *their thinking became futile* and their foolish hearts were darkened. Although they claimed to be wise, they *became fools* and exchanged the glory of the immortal God for images made to look like mortal man and birds and animals and reptiles.

ROMANS 1:20-23, NIV, (emphasis mine)

When we do not acknowledge God, our way of thinking jumps the tracks. We imagine weird and foolish solutions to our problems. Our hearts get dark and we begin to love evil more than good. We become so self-centered that the path of least resistance becomes "our truth." We throw absolutes away and do what is right in our own eyes.

This is what is happening today. Contemporary ideas about manhood have became increasingly deviant and most people don't even realize it. We have lost the code— the truth of God's Word. What used to seem so obvious has become a mystery to many. The creature has rejected the Creator, and no matter how we try to search out our own purpose and meaning apart from God, we will never come to the knowledge of the truth.

THE IMAGE OF A MAN

What is manhood? It is a simple, straightforward question, and the answer should not be as difficult as it has become. But we live in one of the most confused generations in history. Advertising agencies give their picture of what a man is—an open shirt, tight jeans, and an earring. Some ads promise that their cologne will make us a man. Marketing executives know that if they could come up with a product that could furnish a true sense of male identity, they would all be multimillionaires.

Some say that the movie and television industries reflect attitudes and actions that are already prevalent in society but really do not influence us to act a certain way. I doubt if that is true, but in whatever degree the media is a mirror, it is reflecting strange and distorted images of manhood too.

There are the macho men—the Dirty Harrys, the Rambos, and the Schwarzeneggers. Macho men are those who assert their manhood by means of brute force and threats. They try to dominate those around them and consequently destroy and intimidate those who love them. Impoverished men flock to see and cheer on these macho heroes—their concept of what a man should be.

Then there are the Archie Bunker types—the proud urban bigots who imagine they rule their families by constantly belittling them, while everyone ridicules them behind their backs.

Television comedies often portray husbands as half-bumbling idiots or ineffective men who are depending on competent women to help them through life. There are also the world-class wimps like Homer Simpson, the well-meaning, self-centered "klutz" who is constantly outwitted by his children, his wife, and even his dog. This is "family" television.

Then there are the "gender-blenders" like Michael Jackson. *People* magazine reported that when a psychologist asked his seven-year-old nephew, "Is Michael Jackson a boy or a girl?" the boy thought for a moment, then replied, "Both, I think."[1]

Who is a model and example of what it is to be a man in the entertainment world: Eddie Murphy? Mick Jagger? Jay Leno? Michael Bolton? The popular definition of a great man, especially in the entertainment business, is found in how a man looks and acts with little consideration for who he really is. Image and talent completely overshadow any resemblance of character, good or bad.

Is the media the cause or the effect of our distorted image of manhood? Probably both. Media broadcasts a perverted image and establishes it as something to be considered normal. In the absence of biblical influence, we are the product of its powerful effect. As these distorted definitions of a man come to be accepted as valid, our understanding of true manhood deteriorates. And as a society, we are reaping what we have sown.

A SLIPPERY SLOPE

Today many boys are struggling to identify what manhood really is. Young men do not know what it is to be a man, how to be a pillar in the community, how to be a leader, how to treat women, how to be courteous, or how to be confident and secure in who they are. Thousands of young men are growing up without fathers or other significant male role models actively involved in their lives.

Fatherless boys lack the male influence they need to understand what a man is called to be. Fatherless girls grow up with a misunderstanding of how to relate to the opposite gender. There are astounding statistics that show what happens when men do not take the rightful place in the home and in the family. Some have reported that ninety percent of men in prison had no male role-model. Sadly, today over fifty percent of black males are raised by women. More than half of our nation's children will spend some part of their childhood without a father. David Blackenhorn says that fathers are going out of style.[2]

Richard John Neuhaus says, "Millions of children do not know, and will never know, what it means to have a father. More poignantly, they do no know anyone who has a father or is a father.... It takes little imagination to begin to understand the intergenerational consequences of this situation. It is reasonable to ask whether, in all of human history, we have an instance of a large population in which the institution of the family simply disappeared. It is reasonable and ominous, for the answer is almost certainly no. There is no historical precedent supporting the hope that the family, once it has disappeared, can be reconstituted."[3]

In the biblical model of the family, God created fathers.

In the absence of the father, the men in the extended family were to step in to provide male leadership. But that is not happening today. Today, in American society, fathers are not there—indeed, no man is. We have lost the art of manhood, the code to our real meaning and purpose as men. As a consequence, families are disappearing and we are creating a slippery slope for our young boys growing up to be the men of our next generation.

Albert Einstein once said, "The significant problems we face cannot be solved by the same level of thinking that created them." Consequently, we will not get back to true manhood until we find God's perspective.

TRUE MANHOOD

When we define manhood in primarily external terms, as the media often does, we wander far away from its true meaning. But we commonly emphasize external qualities over inner qualities. Mistakenly, we men get our identity and sense of worth from the things we accomplish—the most accounts sold, highest RBI, our annual salary, or our car. We strive to reach such external goals and, consequently, do not build the inner world, which really defines the man.

Ed Cole, president of Christian Men's Network, says, "Real manhood is found within the heart of a man, the 'inner man,' his moral character, the 'real man' that exudes beyond all external devices for the rest of the world to see."[4] If we want to be real men, we must do so internally. Psalms 51:6 says, "Behold, thou desirest truth in the inward parts: and in the hidden part thou shalt make me to know wisdom" (KJV). The Bible also tells us that man looks on externals, but God looks at the heart.

In God's eyes, it is the innermost part of a man that determines what he is.

So, who are real men? Real men are those who live up to a biblical perspective and display the character of Jesus. Their inner character shines through on the outside. They are strong, loving, caring, touching, prayerful, considerate, romantic, selfless, and much more.

There are many role models of "real men" today, each characterized by his own inner qualities. Billy Graham is a man in the true sense of the word because he stands up for what he believes. More importantly, he stands up for God in the face of opposition—Marxists, Communists, atheists, and anarchists. He says what he believes, straight and simple. That takes strength, a mark of a man.

Baseball Hall of Famer Mickey Mantle has not only been a role model to many men and boys, but he has also looked up to other men. Mantle admired Bobby Richardson, a former Yankee player, because he wasn't like the rest of the players—he didn't drink and smoke. Richardson, a seven-time All Star second baseman, was named the Most Valuable Player in the 1960 World Series. He finished second to Mantle in 1962 as the league's Most Valuable Player.[5]

Richardson visited Mantle at the Baylor Hospital in Dallas before Mantle died. Of the meeting, Jim Jones, the religion editor for the *Star-Telegram*, wrote:

Mantle, in the end, found spiritual peace, Richardson said. He told of visiting Mantle at Baylor Hospital in Dallas.

"Mickey had a smile on his face and the first thing he said was, 'Bobby, I've been waiting to tell you something. I want you to know that I've received Christ as my Savior.'"

Richardson wept.[6]

Richardson's wife, Betsy, asked Mickey, "If God were here today, what would you do to convince him he should let you into heaven?" Without hesitation, Mantle quoted John 3:16, "For God so loved the world, that He gave His only begotten Son, that *whoever* believes in Him should not perish, but have eternal life" (emphasis mine).

That day Mickey Mantle became part of *God's* hall of fame. But the true hero is Bobby Richardson, whose first priority was not fame and fortune, but serving God and ministering to others. That is part of being a real man.

Ricky Skaggs and Kirk Whalum are real men. Each man has made a costly decision to honor the Lord in the music business. Ricky is outspoken for God in a world where Christianity is not cool. In the music business, like in most of the entertainment industries, it is cool to be sinful. Ricky has made a choice to sing songs that speak of truth and family values. He is not a preacher nor overly spiritual. Yet, he is clear about his own values, and that, too, is part of being a real man.

Kirk Whalum is a sax player for Whitney Houston and other noted musicians. He played on the recording "I Will Always Love You" and was featured on two cuts from Take Six's 1995 Grammy-winning album *Join the Band.* Four of his albums sold over 125,000 copies. At the age of thirty-seven, when Kirk was at the peak of his career, he was faced with a decision—to sacrifice his commitments at home in order to pursue his music career, or to spend more time with his wife and children and risk losing the momentum in his music career.

"My family gives me a never-ending lesson in unselfishness,..." Kirk says. "Any person committed to being an artist can feel he has to be selfish so he can spend time alone creating. I've had to learn to organize my time so I can put my family first."[7] Kirk quit his full-time position of touring with world-class groups to spend more time with his family.

It is easy to go with the flow, to grab what is handed to us. It is natural to want to take advantage of opportunities that come our way, especially if we have spent a lifetime waiting for them. But it takes conviction, faithfulness, and strength to stick to our priorities and say, "No," as Kirk Whalum did. That is my definition of a real man.

Real manhood is not found in movies and magazines. External gloss alone does not make the man. Real manhood develops in the inward parts. To define true manhood, we must look at the Creator's manual and how God revealed what a man should be in the manhood of Jesus. The Bible says, "To do right honors God; to sin is to despise Him" (Prv 14:2, LB). When we do the right thing, that is manly. When we do the right thing, that is to worship God.

■ ■ ■ ■ ■

TWO

Jesus Is Our Model

The courtyard was completely packed with people from all over the world. It had all the sounds, sights, and smells of a busy marketplace. As in most commercial transactions, the asking price was never the real price. Angrily haggling over money was simply the way business was done in that part of the world. As everyone scurried about, few noticed a man sitting in the corner weaving together pieces of leather. No one paid any attention until he suddenly, though very deliberately, approached the tables with a long whip in his hand.

The leather cords whistled through the air, then loudly cracked. Merchandise and money went flying everywhere. Again the whip cracked. Bird cages were overturned, and doves flew in all directions.

Crack! it sounded again.

His eyes were aflame with anger as he relentlessly slashed his whip to the left and then to the right. "Don't make my Father's house a house of commerce!" he cried with a loud voice. By now tables were being pushed over, and everyone's eyes were on the man with the whip.

"Get out!" he yelled.

The intruder hit the sheep with his self-made whip, and

they scurried into the crowd. The orderly place of business suddenly was thrown into chaos and confusion. The money changers began to feel threatened, realizing they were the targets of this madman. Within a matter of minutes the man had used his whip to drive all the merchants like a herd of cattle from the temple.

The zeal for the house of the Lord that caused Jesus as a boy to linger in the temple asking questions of the teachers now fueled His anger at the merchants and money changers who had turned worship into something trivial and superficial.

A BLUE-COLLAR MESSIAH

The story of the money changers in the temple shows us that, though Jesus was the demonstration of God's love and compassion for the world, He was not an emasculated leader who avoided conflict at all cost. As we learn more about Him, we know that He was not brutish, self-centered, or arrogant. No, Jesus can best be described by the word "common." He was just like us—not a superman, not a wimp—just a regular kind of guy, a common everyday man. But His qualities construct the perfect paradigm for manhood.

There is a tendency to distort the image of Jesus. He is often portrayed in movies as the blond-haired, blue-eyed, Robert Redford type, made up to look a lot better than the average guy. Or many attempt to create Him as a superhero in an effort to overcompensate for many effeminate portrayals.

People who visualize Jesus to be in either of these two extreme categories of manhood have not fully understood the person of Jesus. Jesus was more the average man than anything else. He was subject to life's trials and difficulties, just like you and me. Isaiah 53 contains the prophecy of how the Messiah would bear our grief and sorrows, be pierced for our transgression and crushed for our iniquities. Isaiah also describes how He would appear to us.

He had no beauty or majesty to attract us to him, nothing in his appearance that we should desire him. He was despised and rejected by men, a man of sorrows, and familiar with suffering. Like one from whom men hide their faces he was despised, and we esteemed him not.

ISAIAH 53:2-3, NIV

Jesus suffered just as we sometimes do. He was rejected, despised, and even hated. He was mistreated and falsely accused. He was promoted as king in Jerusalem and then not only dismissed in the public's eyes, but hunted as a fugitive and killed. Jesus was a real man. He was like us in every way, yet he was also divine. It doesn't matter how we portray Jesus externally. Jesus' manhood was an internal, spiritual thing.

Unfortunately, Christians' understanding of Jesus is more akin to Greek *mythology* than to biblical *theology*. The gods that were created and worshiped by the Greeks were neither eternal nor omnipotent. They were more like comic book characters—Superman, Spiderman, or the Power Rangers. They were magnified images of humanity with superhuman powers. Hercules was the strongest and most celebrated of the heroes of classical mythology. As an infant, this superhero strangled two serpents that were placed in his cradle to destroy him. His life was dedicated to fighting monsters and bad guys with his supernatural powers. He was a figment of someone's imagination who also proclaimed him as a god.

In the early days of the church, a number of spurious gospel accounts tried to diminish the humility of Jesus' genuine humanity. But the documents were rejected by the church and by those who had been eyewitnesses to the mighty words and deeds of Jesus.

Jesus was God who became an average, everyday man—a blue-collar kind of guy. In this way He became the example of what we as men should be. If He had been extraordinarily human, a Hercules endued with special advantages, then He could not be the standard for every man. The miracles He performed while on earth confirmed His deity, but the emphasis of His life was that He emptied Himself of divine power and glory. He performed miracles by means of relying on the Father to act on His behalf, just as each of us in our own faith has to do.

JESUS, *THE* REAL MAN

Jesus is not only the perfect representation to us of the Father, but He was also the perfect example of a real man. His inner qualities shone in His earthly greatness. He was responsible, disciplined, and honest. He was committed, genuine, and down-to-earth in His spirituality. He relied on His Father and took time to get away with Him to worship. Worship and time alone with God was the mainstay of His life on earth.

To be like Him, we must know what it means to be a man in terms of internal character. But we cannot be the man we were created to be without understanding how to worship God with all that we are. Here are some attributes of Jesus that lead the way for our becoming real men. One of these attributes is the ability and willingness to enter into true worship of God.

1. The Real Man Always Comes Through. Real men are responsible—to God, to their families, to their communities, to all those who count on them. No other character quality is more fundamental to great men.

Jesus' greatness as the Son of Man was not due to the fact that He formerly sat as Creator and Ruler of the universe, but because He demonstrated the quality of being a responsible man. Jesus showed responsibility when He told John to look after Mary, His mother (see John 19:27). He also took responsibility to feed the five thousand men who had come to hear Him speak. He cared for their physical needs (see John 6:1-14). He demonstrated care and concern when He told Peter, "Tend my lambs" (Jn 21:15).

John 15:10 says, "If ye keep my commandments, ye shall abide in my love; even as I have kept my Father's commandments, and abide in his love" (KJV). And He commands (not suggests) that we do the same. He said *keep my commandments as I have kept my Father's*. If He asked us to do this, He will certainly provide us with the ability to follow through. He would not ask us to do something we are not able to do.

The Holy Spirit is drawing men from all over the world to be modern-day disciples of Jesus, Who, near the end of His earthly life, prayed to His Father: "I have revealed you to those whom you gave me out of the world. They were yours; you gave them to me and they have obeyed your word" (Jn 17:6, NIV). To be a disciple—to be a real man after the image of *The* Real Man—means we keep God's commandments and come through for those who are counting on us.

2. The Real Man Knows Who He Is. Jesus was a secure man who knew exactly who He was and what He was supposed to do. He never acted hastily or in retaliation because of deep-rooted insecurity or a poor self-image. He knew His purpose. Jesus was comfortable with being the Son of God and the Son of Man.

The voice from heaven trumpeted, "This is my Beloved Son, in whom I am well-pleased" (Mt 3:17, NKJV). That phrase was made up of two well-known passages from the Old Testament. First, "Thou art my Son" comes from Psalm 2, which describes the reign on earth of the kingly Messiah. Second, the servant with whom the Lord is "well-pleased" comes from the chapters of Isaiah that describe the Lord's Suffering Servant. What the Father was saying to the Son was that He was to be both the kingly Messiah of Psalm 2 and the Suffering Servant of the Book of Isaiah. No one ever imagined the two could be the same person, but Jesus knew both roles: Who He was and what He came to do.

Satan tempted Christ in both areas—Who He really was and what He came to do. "If you are the Son of God..." Satan would say each time. Satan suggested that He make bread for Himself to satisfy His hunger, cast Himself from the temple to gain popularity, or bow down to Satan in exchange for the kingdoms of the world. In each case Jesus was tempted to gain His kingdom the easy way. The test was this: Was He willing to accept the role of the Suffering Servant and go the route of the cross?

Satan also tempts us in both areas—who we believe we are and what we decide to do. Being faithful to our position and purpose is characteristic of great men. All of us, at times, are tempted to forget or set aside who we are and what we are called to be. That is always the first step toward sin. Jesus knew Who He was—a kingly Messiah— and what He was called to be—the Suffering Servant. In the wilderness and throughout His life and ministry, He refused to deny either at any cost.

3. The Real Man Is Always in Control of Himself. Awesome power was at Jesus' immediate disposal. This was made apparent in His hometown at the very beginning of His ministry. Jesus went into the synagogue and began to read about the Messiah from the scroll. Jesus said to them, "Today this scripture is fulfilled in your hearing."

All the people in the synagogue were furious when they heard this. They got up, drove him out of the town, and took him to the brow of the hill on which the town was built, in order to throw him down the cliff. But he walked right through the crowd and went on his way.

LUKE 4:28-30, NIV

Jesus could have dramatically proven Who He was. After all, they were going to kill Him. Jesus escaped, not because He was a coward, but because it wasn't His time.

Though He had unlimited power at His disposal, His power was under control and submitted to the Father's purpose for Him. Throughout the Gospels, Jesus' greatness is revealed in His self-restraint. Jesus often walked away from conflicts He knew He could win. When Peter was determined to fight those who had come to arrest Jesus in the garden, the Lord said to him, "Do you think that I cannot pray to my Father, and He will not provide Me with more than twelve legions of angels?" (Mt 26:53, NKJV). Nevertheless, He suffered many humiliating indignities—the last of which was hanging on the cross, enduring a slow, agonizing death for you and me. He refused to use power available to Him to save Himself when it did not serve God's purpose. Self-restraint is the mark of a really great man, and none displayed it more clearly than Jesus.

4. The Real Man Is an Intercessor. The man Jesus is in heaven interceding for those He loves. "Therefore, holy brothers, who share in the heavenly calling, fix your thoughts on Jesus, the apostle and high priest whom we confess" (Heb 3:1, NIV). Jesus is the priest that covers His family, the church, in prayer, standing in the gap on behalf of the sons and daughters, brothers and sisters, for whom He is responsible. He prays for us always, interceding for our well-being.

Many times people don't realize how intimately acquainted Jesus is with the problems we face. He knows what we are going through as one who has been through it Himself. He was sinless and perfect, yes, but He also experienced the weakness and pain of humanity and the seduction of Satan's temptation. Jesus knows we need an intercessor. Hebrews 4:15 says, "For we have not a high priest which cannot be touched with the feeling of our infirmities; but *was in all points tempted like as we are*, yet without sin" (KJV, emphasis mine). Jesus faced, in some form or another, the same temptations that confront each of us. He has felt the hurts, the failures, the disappointments that are common to all men. He knows what we go through because He has been there.

Though He was tempted, Jesus did not sin. To sin, we have to consent to the temptation. Someone once said that you cannot stop the birds from flying over your head, but you can keep them from nesting in your hair. You cannot stop thoughts from coming into your mind, but you don't have to let them stay and build a fort. Ephesians 4:27 says, "Do not give the devil an opportunity."

Temptation is like the lying salesman who tries to get us to buy a defective product. The salesman never tells us about the consequences of the temptation, only the promises of a moment of pleasure. If we buy in, along with the moments of gratification we reap the horrible consequences of the sin. The payback for sin is death— death to our relationships, death to our finances, death to our health and, even, death to our spiritual health. All sin is basically self-centered. It puts us first, and it will always hurt others. But we are not left helpless. Because Jesus has been where we are now, we can have confidence that He is able to help us in times of temptation.

> For we do not have a high priest who cannot sympathize with our weaknesses, but one who has been tempted in all things as we are, yet without sin. Let us therefore draw near with confidence to the throne of grace, that we may receive mercy and may find grace to help in time of need.
>
> HEBREWS 4:15-16

> Therefore, in all things He was obligated to be made like His brethren, that He might be a merciful and faithful High Priest in things pertaining to God, to make propitiation for the sins of the people. For in that He Himself has suffered, being tempted, He is able to aid those who are tempted.
>
> HEBREWS 2:17-18, NKJV

Concerning all the problems and temptations we face in this life, Jesus has, so to speak, *been there and overcome that*. Now He intercedes for us with the Father concerning both our greatest and smallest needs. Jesus, *The* Real Man, is a constant intercessor for His family.

He is able to save forever those who draw near to God through Him, since He always lives to make intercession for them.

HEBREWS 7:25

5. The Real Man Is a Wholehearted Worshiper. Jesus demonstrated the most wholehearted worship in the New Testament, in fact, in the whole Bible. He was a little too extreme for the superficial religious people of His day— and ours. But He is, nevertheless, the model or prototype of what we should be as worshipers.

After Jesus commissioned the seventy disciples to go out two by two evangelizing and healing, they returned with the good report and said, "Lord, even the demons are subject to us in your name" (Lk 10:17). The Lord responded, "Nevertheless do not rejoice in this, that the spirits are subject to you, but rejoice that your names are recorded in heaven." Scripture tells us that at that very moment "he rejoiced greatly in the Holy Spirit" (Lk 10:20-21).

The word *rejoiced* in this passage comes from two Greek words that can mean to jump or leap under violent emotion. Jesus worshiped in this way in the presence of His disciples. Do we freely express ourselves in worship before those to whom we are godly influences—our children, our wives, our friends, the younger men? How many church leaders jump emotionally in front of those they are discipling? How many men worship the Lord in total abandonment in the presence of others?

I remember a men's meeting we had at our church, Metroplex Covenant Church, in Colleyville, Texas. Sunday morning the pastor encouraged all the men, thirteen years old and up, to come to church on Sunday night "wearing your suspenders and tennis shoes. You may need them," he teased. "LaMar is teaching us about manly worship."

That night there were about three hundred men present. I wasn't prepared for what happened. As I began to lead the worship with a song, I was tremendously impacted by the volume and the baritone roar of three hundred men singing with all their might. One man in his work boots and red suspenders—a man I had never seen move much in public worship—was leaping across the back of the sanctuary with his arms flinging in the air. What a sight!

The men were excited and began to clap and jump as the praise increased. In fact, at one point some of them spontaneously began to march in a single line around the sanctuary. Some of the musicians, instruments in hand, joined them. They clapped and roared with spontaneous worship.

I looked around to see some of the younger men crying. The sons had perhaps never seen their fathers worship like this, and they were touched deeply. They were moved to tears by the presence of God and by seeing their dads worship freely. One man came up to me at the end of the service and said, "This is better than a football game."

When a sports fan says worship is better than football, you know you are in a worship renewal.

The word got out in the church community that the men had freely worshiped and encountered the presence of the Lord. The church was full of excitement and anticipation over what the men would do in the next Sunday morning worship service. Many were disappointed to see most of the men return to their stuffy, quiet, religious roles again.

What was the difference between the men's meeting and a Sunday morning worship service? Perhaps the men were uneasy about worshiping freely with their wives and children present. Perhaps they were operating under the assumption that, as leaders and as men, they should be more conservative in their worship.

Are we like that? Is the rigidness of our Sunday morning worship service for the sake of visitors who may be present? If the visitors want a dead religious service with little extravagant worship, they can go to a number of stoic and conservative churches. But real men do not want mere religion; they want to know and experience the power of God's presence and witness Christians who are alive in their worship. They want to be like Jesus, who didn't hold back from *rejoicing greatly* in the presence of His disciples. Jesus was an example to those He led of how they should worship. And He is a model for us. It is important, then, that we understand the meaning and purpose of worship and how a real man begins to worship like Jesus.

■　■　■　■　■

THREE

The Inner World of Worship

There is a stereotypical perception that men have about women—that they are sensitive, emotional, and, at times, irrational. Women are not, we men sometimes think, "normal" like we are. But Jesus said before we pull the splinter out of the eye of another (in this case, women) we must first behold the log in our own.

Men are generally analytical and structured, and often we bring these attributes to our worship. We like formal, systematic worship because it is very predictable. We tend to be uncomfortable without order and control. Consequently, there is little chance for the kind of spontaneity that might appear uncool or "irrational." For these reasons many men cling tenaciously to the safety of ritual and tradition in our worship services.

Brian Doerksen, a well-known Vineyard worship leader and fellow Western Canadian, spoke at a worship institute in Seattle about his ritualistic upbringing:

> As a child I was told not to cry and taught that it was wrong to show emotions. "To show emotions is a sign of weakness," my dad had told me. The church taught my dad to be a skeptic about many things.

Thankfully, he has recovered. We were very isolated. Mennonites kept to themselves. We were exclusive, and I grew up disconnected from the rest of the Body of Christ. We wanted systems that kept us the same, far away from change.[1]

Like Brian, many men have been taught from childhood to hide emotions and to avoid appearing "overly sensitive" even in the most sensitive of situations. This kind of training has left us men with little room to express who we are, to show our real feelings spontaneously and freely. Yet, as we look at the subject of worship, we find that, by definition, the act of worship has an external component. True worship is an offering, an outward expression of a devotion that begins inside. Though worship begins internally, it finds fulfillment externally. True worship requires the expression of our emotions. It cannot be sustained in an environment of ritual and tradition, of strict systems and control. Neither can we attain it until we remove the log from our eye.

INNER-WORLD WORSHIP

The outer world, our public world, is the dimension of our lives that is on stage for everyone to see. It consists of work, play, possessions, and a host of acquaintances who make up our social circle. For some, this visible dimension becomes the central focus of our lives. When this happens, we live in the external, and all that has meaning and purpose in life for us exists in that realm.

The inner, private world is more emotional and spiritual in nature, however. It is the place where choices and values are determined, where solitude and reflection are pursued. It is where prayers and confessions are made. It is here that our consciences are rooted. This inner sanctum of the heart is the hotbed or incubator for communion with God, the place where worship begins. If this part of our lives is not carefully cultivated, our worship will be, at best, external, ritualistic, and passionless.

The inner world is to be the place of peace and tranquility. It is where the Spirit of God comes to make self-disclosure, to impart wisdom, to give affirmation or rebuke, to provide encouragement, and to give directions and guidance. Very often, this inner life is cheated and neglected by the unceasing demands of the external world. When we neglect our private inner world, we then, by default, permit ourselves to be shaped by outer influences. Beware the barrenness of an overly busy outer world. It will rob us of spiritual genuineness and integrity.

Unfortunately, it is often assumed in church circles that the most publicly active person is also the most privately spiritual. That is obviously naive, but promotion of people in the church on the basis of external image betrays the fact that, too often, church members place little value on cultivating the inner world.

In reality, those most active in public worship may not be engaged in the most spiritual worship. Those who are expressive externally may not necessarily be worshiping with much depth. Their private world of worship may not have been developed. We all need to be encouraged to express our worship outwardly, but that is not the most important goal.

THE GOAL OF WORSHIP

Worship is an expression of dedication to God. It is devotion and adoration to the One who created us and saved us. Worship always requires sacrifice—the giving of one's allegiance and of one's self. Praise can occur even when motives are wrong and self-serving agendas exist. But when true worship occurs, the focus is completely on the One we adore and venerate.

Romans 12:1 gives us a definition of worship. "Therefore, I urge you, brothers, in view of God's mercy, to offer your bodies as living sacrifices, holy and pleasing to God—this is your spiritual act of worship" (NIV). An offering is a free-will gift. When we pray, read the Bible, or confess our faith, there is an expectation that we are going to get something back from God. But worship is the spiritual act of freely giving something that costs us—it is a sacrifice. It is giving to God without expecting a return.

Many Christians equate worship with only external expressions—singing, clapping, and playing musical instruments. We assume that worship occurs during the musical part of the service. We erroneously believe that when the singing stops, so does the worship. But worship is not confined to the church building on Sunday morning. We are either worshiping or not worshiping each minute of every day. Worship is offering sacrificially our attitudes and actions to God. "Whatever you do," says Paul, "work at it with all your heart, as working for the Lord, not for men" (Col 3:23, NIV). No matter what we do, we can do it for the Lord as an act of worship before Him. Our entire lives can be an act of worship.

God created us as spiritual beings. It has been said that we live in a body, we have emotions, but we *are* spiritual beings. Worship, as does life itself, proceeds from within—from the inner world to the outer. If the visible dimension is not rooted in—and springing forth from—that which is taking place in our inner, private world, then our life and worship is only a shell of what it could be and what it was meant to be.

How can we cultivate an inner world that brings forth meaningful worship? Proverbs 4:23 says, "Watch over your heart with all diligence, for from it flows the springs of life" (NASB). The Lord is obviously concerned that the heart be protected from external influences that might jeopardize its integrity. He is concerned about its strength and development. We must make a choice if we are to keep our hearts in tune with God. Our hearts must be constantly protected and maintained. Paul talked about this in Romans 12:2: "Do not be conformed to this world—this age, fashioned after and adapted to its external, superficial customs" (AMP).

Our inner world is like a garden. What does it look like? Is it well-groomed or overgrown with all kinds of weeds? When the inner world is neglected, we begin to lose our perspective on spiritual reality until, finally, we can no longer see things from God's perspective. When we place the highest priority on the quality of our hearts, we are increasing not only the quality of our character and life but the quality of our worship.

THE PRIORITY OF WORSHIP

For every Christian, the act of worship should assume a place of highest importance in our lives because Scripture has made it a priority. "Fear God, and give him glory," the angel says in Revelation 14:7, "because the hour of his judgment has come; and worship him who made the heaven and the earth and sea and springs of waters." The supreme duty of all creatures, including man, for time and eternity, is to worship the Creator. Jesus said, "You shall worship the Lord your God, and serve him only" (Mt 4:10, NASB). A. W. Tozer said God sent his Son so that "He might restore to us the missing jewel, the jewel of worship: that we might come back and learn to do again that which we were created to do in the first place—worship the Lord in the beauty of holiness, to spend our time in awesome wonder and adoration of God, feeling and expressing it. We're here to be worshipers first and workers only second."[2]

Our first obligation to our Creator and Savior is to worship Him. We are told this in both the Old and the New Testaments. In the first commandment of the Law under the Old Covenant, God tells us to give Him first place in our lives: "You shall have no other gods before me" (Ex

20:3, NASB). God is to be our top priority and we are to worship no other gods before Him. Worship is also the first and greatest commandment of the New Covenant: "You shall love the Lord your God with all your heart, with all your soul, and with all your mind. This is the first and great commandment" (Mt 22:36-38, NKJV.) Whenever we gather together in a Christian meeting, then, with God as our priority, our chief aim should be to worship Him.

The Bible tells us that every believer in every nation is to worship God. "Who shall not fear thee, O Lord, and glorify thy name? For thou only art holy; for all nations shall come and worship before thee; for thy judgments are made manifest" (Rv 15:4, KJV). This call establishes worship as the universal priority. Indeed, all history will culminate in an eternal worship service in the presence of our glorious Lord: "And I heard a great multitude and as the sound of many waters and as the sound of mighty peals of thunder, saying, 'Hallelujah! For the Lord our God Almighty reigns. Let us rejoice and be glad and give glory to Him...'" (Rv 19:6,7a).

If we as Christians are to be worshipers first, is it not important, then, for us to understand the nature of worship and to know more about *how* to worship? Once again, Jesus, our model, has shown us the way.

THE FUNDAMENTALS OF WORSHIP

In prayer Jesus taught us to worship. "And He said to them, When you pray, say: Our Father *Who is in heaven,* hallowed be Your name" (Lk 11:2, AMP). In this prayer, Jesus shows us that before we petition God in prayer, we should worship Him—"Hallowed be your name"—not because of "what" He can do for us but for "Who" He is.

Worship is centered on God's person, not His performance. Unlike praise, which often declares what God has done in our behalf, worship focuses on God's person and character. Worship is transcendent. It looks at the person of our praise and not the benefits of knowing Him. This is the selfless nature of worship.

We might best examine this selflessness in our worship of God by considering selflessness in earthly relationships. A man comes home from a busy day at work. He hasn't had much time to be with his wife and children during the week. But now it's Friday, and his plans are to spend the whole weekend with those he loves so much. With briefcase and jacket in hand he bursts in the door.

"I'm home, everyone. Dad's home!" he announces with excitement.

"Oh, hi, Dad," mutters his son without taking his eyes off the television.

A stampede of little bodies runs past him. "Look out, we're playing chase."

Then he hears a voice from the kitchen, "Honey, is that you?"

"Yes, dear."

"Did you pick up John?" his wife asks.

"Oh, no, I forgot," he sighs.

"Well, go get him from football practice," his wife orders. "Did you cash the check from work?"

"No."

"Well, go cash it!" she barks. "Then please get this screen door fixed and, for heaven's sake, take that garbage out."

"Yes, dear," the man says with great disappointment. Turning to leave he stops and looks toward the kitchen and whispers, "I just wanted a hug." His heart is crushed. He just wanted to be loved.

This story paints a picture of how we might relate to Christ and poses a number of questions for us. Did the wife in this story marry her spouse because she fell in love with him as a person, or for what he could do for her? Did she see her husband only as the chauffeur for the children, or as the repairman, and garbage collector? Or did she see him, first and foremost, as the person she loves?

How do we look at Christ? Is He to us merely the One who picks us up when we are down, the Provider for our home, and the Repairman who keeps things together? Is Jesus only our Savior, Healer, Deliverer, and Provider? Or is He the person to whom we gave our lives—the One that we love so dearly? Worship focuses on the person of Christ, not what He can do for us.

Worship is love expressed. It is an attitude of the heart—an attitude "given wings" in adoration, praise, and thanksgiving. It is not merely singing, bowing, dancing, or lifting hands. Those, at best, are the mere external expressions of love. True worship is the expression of an inner attitude, and that inner attitude determines the integrity of our worship.

Worship is personal and individual, and cannot be done for us by others. Ministers and worship leaders can never be surrogate worshipers. Because we sing songs and follow the worship leaders at the front of the church service does not mean we are worshiping. If worship does not take place in our hearts, it is not true worship.

Worship is an interactive encounter between the Creator and His human creatures. Singing His attributes glorifies and magnifies Him in the eyes and ears of men and angels.

THE RIGHT PLACE TO WORSHIP

Since the coming of Christ, true worship occurs in or from the spirit and no longer consists of mere external forms of religious systems.

Yet a time is coming and has now come when the true worshipers will worship the Father in spirit and truth, for they are the kind of worshipers the Father seeks. God is spirit, and his worshipers must worship in spirit and in truth.

JOHN 4:23-24, NIV

Humans have obscured great deficiencies in their true inner spiritual condition by focusing on controversies over forms of worship. The Samaritan woman illustrates this. She told Jesus that "our fathers" had worshiped on Mount Gerizim, which the Samaritans insisted was the holy and right place of worship (Jn 4:20.) She also emphasized its importance as a tradition that had been passed down from generation to generation. "Our fathers worshiped here," she told Jesus. But Jesus responded to her in this way.

> Believe me, woman, a time is coming when you will worship the Father neither on this mountain nor in Jerusalem. You Samaritans worship what you do not know; we worship what we do know, for salvation is from the Jews. Yet a time is coming and now has come when the true worshipers will worship the Father in spirit and truth, for they are the kind of worshipers the Father seeks. God is spirit, and his worshipers must worship in spirit and in truth.
>
> JOHN 4:21-24, NIV

Since the coming of Christ, we can offer acceptable worship to God anywhere. God does not prefer our worship be expressed in one place or another. It is our own religious traditions that put emphasis on the external and public places of worship.

The focus is not upon the "state of the place" where we worship God, but upon the "state of heart" in which we worship Him. Old Testament worship was ceremonial.

The worshipers focused on many outward rituals and procedures. But the way of worship which Christ has instituted is spiritual and internal, refined from those external rites and ceremonies of Old Testament worship. Those who returned to Judaism after becoming Christians were said to have begun in the spirit and ended in the flesh (see Galatians 3:3). Such is the difference between Old Testament and New Testament institutions. It is required of all who worship God that they worship Him in spirit and in truth. We must heed the power more than the form, and draw near to God with a true heart.

Today, most denominations worship in a traditional way, a manner passed down for many generations. Worship is "institutionalized" in some attempt at quality control. But external conventions of worship do not guarantee genuine spiritual worship. In a very formalized system of worship, people are able to follow the procedures whether they know the Lord personally or not. To illustrate this, a poll was taken outside of a Christian church. The question was asked, "How do you know that you will go to heaven?" Some of the answers were: "I've been a good person; I've been attending this church for forty-five years; I give to charities and to this church." Only a handful said, "Because Christ died for me, and I have given my life to Him." The rest had no personal faith in or connection with Christ, and yet they were placing great trust in their form of worship. Do we have more faith in our external expressions of our worship or in our inner relationship with the Lord?

God wants men to be right on the inside. Worship does

not begin with external expression. It begins in the inner private world of our heart. We must leave the safety of our external ritual and tradition, and worship God from the inner garden of our heart. When this garden is well manicured and cared for, it bears fruit suitable for the rich table of the King of Kings, and we are able to worship God in spirit and in truth.

■ ■ ■ ■ ■

FOUR

The Man Without Excuse

What a lovely meal it was! The reception was at the home of Simon. He was a Pharisee—one of the religious conservatives who resisted the godless influences of Greek culture the Romans had brought to Jerusalem with them. You could always spot a Pharisee by his religious garb. They were a strict religious society who kept the laws more precisely than anyone else. Consequently, they felt they were better and holier than anyone else. The Pharisees were organized followers of the scribes, who were experts in interpreting Scripture. A member had to strictly adhere to the Law, oral or written. They despised those they did not consider their equals and never interacted with a person who was not a Pharisee. They were extreme in their separatism and formalized in their beliefs.

The Pharisees bitterly opposed Jesus' teachings with every ounce of their self-righteous pride. "Unless your righteousness surpasses that of the Pharisees you will certainly not enter the kingdom of heaven," Jesus had said. Who knows why Simon invited Jesus to this dinner party?

Suddenly the door burst open. There stood a woman,

who looked at Jesus. Her eyes were red, and her dress identified her as one of the local prostitutes. Jesus, in the room with a group of Pharisees, was already in an awkward situation. Now the woman's presence added to the Pharisees' tension.

A good Pharisee would not allow himself to be seen with or to touch such a person, much less have a close association with her. And not just because she was a sinner, but also because she was a *woman!* The Sanhedrin, a group of religious leaders made up of Pharisees, scribes, and Sadducees, was the quintessential "ole boys' club." They not only considered themselves superior because of their traditional conservatism, but also because they were guys. This was a woman invading their party.

Without an invitation or a word from the host, the woman went over to where Jesus was reclining at the table and fell to her knees behind Him. She was weeping and she wet His feet with her tears and wiped them with her hair.

Imagine how you would feel if a woman interrupted one of your business lunches telling everyone how good you had been to her. It wouldn't make a very good impression on your friends—and neither did it impress the Pharisees. Simon thought to himself that if Jesus were a true prophet of God, He would not let this sinner touch Him. But Jesus read his thoughts.

"Simon," Jesus said to his host, "I have something to tell you."

"Tell me, teacher," Simon replied respectfully, not knowing Jesus saw his thoughts.

"Two men owed money to the same bank," Jesus began. "One owed an equivalent of a year and a half's wages. The other owed less than two months' wages. Neither of them could repay the bank. Consequently, the bank forgave both their loans. Which of them would be more appreciative?"

"I guess the one who had the greater debt canceled," Simon replied.

"Correct," Jesus said. "Do you see this woman?"

See her! Simon must have thought. *We haven't been able to take our eyes off her!* She was now pouring expensive perfume on His feet. The whole room was beginning to smell. Jesus said to Simon:

> I came into your house; you gave me no water for my feet, but she has wet my feet with her tears, and wiped them with her hair. You gave me no kiss; but she, since the time I came in, has not ceased to kiss my feet. You did not anoint my head with oil, but she anointed my feet with perfume. For this reason I say to you, her sins, which are many, have been forgiven, for she loved much; but he who is forgiven little, loves little.
>
> LUKE 7:44-47

Then He said to the woman, "Your sins have been forgiven. Go in peace."

Jesus could have written a book on how to offend a Pharisee. (Some might say that He did—and we call it the New Testament.) He not only affirmed His association with this low-class woman, but He allowed her to follow Him into Simon's house, making them all "technically" unclean, according to the Law. Then He forgave her sins against God—just like that!

One of the most amazing things about this story is that Jesus' comments to Simon reveal to us a great truth about worship: that Jesus expected the same kind of worship and devotion from Simon and the Pharisees' "ole boys' club" as He received from the sinful woman. In fact, this is only one of the biblical accounts of Jesus rebuking the Pharisees for their unwillingness to worship Him in spirit and in truth. The story of His entrance into Jerusalem gives us an even clearer picture of what Jesus expects of those who truly worship Him.

UNORTHODOX WORSHIP

Five days before His crucifixion, Jesus rode into Jerusalem not on a horse, the prestigious mount of a general or head of state, but on a donkey, a mere creature of service. Christ was coming as a King into Jerusalem, but there were no trumpets announcing His arrival, only the shouts of the believers who heralded His presence. This was the prelude to His Passion.

A very large crowd spread their cloaks on the road, while others cut branches from the trees and spread them on the road. The crowds that went ahead of him and those that followed shouted, "Hosanna to the Son of David!" "Blessed is he who comes in the name of the Lord!" "Hosanna in the highest!" When Jesus entered Jerusalem, the whole city was stirred and asked, "Who is this?" The crowds answered, "This is Jesus, the prophet from Nazareth in Galilee."

MATTHEW 21:8-11, NIV

The Passover would be on the fourteenth day of the month, and this was the tenth, the day on which the Law appointed that the paschal lamb should be taken up and set apart for the sacrifice that would be offered on the Passover. On that day, therefore, Christ, our sacrificial Lamb, was publicly honored as the Messiah and King.

These simple followers of Christ—none with degrees, titles, or honor—spread their clothing on the ground before Jesus, showing their submission to Christ as His subjects. They also cut down the palm branches and laid them in the road; or waved the palms as the Jews did at the Feast of Tabernacles. These were symbols of victory, liberty, and joy.

The shouts of "Hosanna" welcomed the kingdom of Christ, wishing it prosperity and success. With their shouts "Hosanna in the highest," they were saying literally, *Praise God to the highest degree!*

The whole city was moved with wonder. "What's going on?" they were probably saying. Others were filled with joy because for hundreds of years all Israel had been waiting for a Messiah-King, the Son of David who would restore the kingdom.

The scribes were incensed at this outpouring of praise and filled with envy and indignation. Even though they could not deny Jesus' wonderful miracles, He didn't fit within the narrow confines of their presuppositions. Consequently, they opposed Him and His teachings. They had created for themselves a system of external religious practices that was formalized and rigid. This was the chief vice of the scribes and Pharisees: they had reduced religion and worship to something so mechanical that the heart and passion of worship were extinguished. They held on to the old ways, the tradition of their elders. When God moved in a new way, it did not fit in their system. The scribes and Pharisees stood with arms folded and refused to participate.

> But when the chief priests and the teachers of the law saw the wonderful things he did and the children shouting in the temple area, "Hosanna to the Son of David," they were indignant. "Do you hear what these children are saying?" they asked him. "Yes," replied Jesus, "Have you never read, 'From the lips of children and infants you have ordained praise'?"
>
> MATTHEW 21:15-16, NIV

Jesus not only allowed this extravagant and demonstrative display of praise and exaltation, He rebuked those who opposed it. And Jesus went on to tell them that God had ordained this unorthodox expression of praise.

The Pharisees, of course, objected:

Some of the Pharisees from among the multitude said unto him, Master, rebuke thy disciples. And he answered and said unto them, I tell you that, if these should hold their peace, the stones would immediately cry out.

LUKE 19:39-40, KJV

The Pharisees were uncomfortable with this display of celebration and tried to stop it. One of Jesus' denunciations of the Pharisees was this:

Woe to you, scribes and Pharisees, hypocrites, because you shut off the kingdom of heaven from men; for you do not enter in yourselves, nor do you allow those who are entering to go in.

MATTHEW 23:13, NASB

I hate to admit it, but today some men have the same tendencies as did the Pharisees. Men are often uncomfortable with extravagant praise. Not only do we not enter in ourselves but we try to stop others from demonstrating their worship outwardly. We like things orderly, systematized, and controlled. Left to our own devices, as were the scribes and Pharisees, we will turn the love of God and the worship of God into something scholastic, unemotional, and, at all costs, dignified.

But Jesus expected the Pharisees (who might be considered the extreme example of male reluctance) to take part in expressive worship, to pull off their pretty robes and throw them in the street, to wave palm branches, and to praise God in the highest—in the strongest way they knew how.

Many men today might say, *Well, I'm just not like that!* Perhaps the Pharisees could have said the same thing. It was not, however, a matter of what *the worshipers* were like, but Who was present and what *He* was like. "If you don't praise Me," He said, "the rocks will cry out." Certainly, the scribes and Pharisees had their reasons for standing there with their arms folded, their disapproval evident. But, judging by Jesus' response, they had no excuse.

EXCUSES, EXCUSES!

A young boy, when asked by his teacher where his homework was, replied, "The dog ate it." Some of our excuses for withholding ourselves from God probably sound just as unlikely to Him. In fact they are more unrealistic to Him because He sees and knows all things. Men have many reasons why we should be excused from being wholehearted, extravagant worshipers. I have heard some whoppers in the twenty years I have been ministering on worship. Here are a few that I have most often heard:

1. "I've never done that before!" When being challenged to consider new forms of worship, whether it is a new expression of biblical worship or merely singing more contemporary songs, some have said, "We have never done that before!" So what does that mean? It does not fit into our system of worship? Is our worship so formalized, crystallized, and systematized that we are not open to new things the Lord may want us to consider? The next time I hear, "We've never done that before," I may respond, "So change!" Christianity is not a destination, it is a journey. Maturation is a process of transformation. The Christian life is a process of change—of dying to self, of applying the Word of God to our lives, of living a life of greater discipline. Traditional, systematic, codified religion resists change because the worshiper's identity is received from the form of worship, but real Christianity requires personal transformation that is a result of a dynamic relationship with Christ.

2. "I've got other priorities." Giving is a form of worship that shows the depth of our passion and devotion to God. But oftentimes we hold back in giving of our financial resources because we have priorities of our own. Consider this passage in Luke:

> As he looked up, Jesus saw the rich putting their gifts into the temple treasury. He also saw a poor widow put in two very small copper coins. "I tell you the truth," he said, "this poor widow has put in more than all the others. All these people gave their gifts out of their wealth; but she out of her poverty put in all she had to live on."
>
> LUKE 21:1-4, NIV

The widow put two mites (two-fifths of a cent) into the offering plate. Jesus noticed what she had given. He also saw that the rich had given only out of their surplus, whereas the woman had given the money she was to live on. Today some people say they would give more if they had more money. Not so. The more we make, the more committed we have to be to give a full tithe.

Face the facts, men often have control of and access to more money than do women. But as men we often say, "But I've got bills; I've got responsibilities; I've got dreams, goals, investment opportunities...." We put our own priorities first. Jesus looked at the rich men, who were somewhat like today's affluent businessmen with large amounts of discretionary income. Jesus didn't necessarily say that they had to give all that they had, but He denounced them for their lack of passion. He expected the same devotion.

3. "I'm very busy right now." Jesus told a story about a man who wanted to invite many people to an extravagant dinner (see Luke 14:16-23). In the hour that the meal was ready he sent out his servant to say to the men that had been invited, "Come, for everything is ready." They all began to make excuses.

"I'm sorry, I just purchased some property that I have to go see. Please have me excused," one person said.

Another man said, "I bought five yoke of oxen that I have to inspect. Excuse me."

A third man said, "I have just been married and I really cannot come right now."

The servant returned and reported what the men had said. The master of the house became very angry and told his servant to go and bring in the poor, disabled, blind, and lame. And they came, yet there was more room. The master said, "Go out into the highways and hedges and urge and constrain them to come in so the house will be filled." The master said, "None of those that were invited will taste of this meal."

The men who had been invited to participate made excuses and were then rejected. Jesus said, "If anyone comes to me and does not hate his father and mother, his wife and children, his brothers and sisters—yes, even his own life—he cannot be my disciple. And anyone who does not carry his cross and follow me cannot be my disciple" (Lk 14:26-27, NIV).

What excuses do we make to not do what Christ has invited us to do? Do we make excuses when it is time to worship?

4. "What will other people think?" Men are so self-conscious! We want to look good to others. This desire is rooted in pride and in our poor self-esteem. Jesus said to the men He was teaching, "If anyone would come after me, he must deny himself and take up his cross and follow me. For whoever wants to save his life will lose it, but whoever loses his life for me will find it" (Mt 16:24-25, NIV).

In order to commit ourselves fully to God, we men must "deny ourselves." We must deny our flesh and what it wants. As leaders of our family and the church, we need to allow ourselves to be transformed by dying to our own wants and desires, and to come alive to our commitment to God. That is the opposite of making ourselves look good. We must forsake our pride and our concern about what other people will think. Pride will kill not only our worship but our spiritual relationship with Christ.

I once heard someone observe that real masculinity involves a willingness to remain committed to loved ones no matter what circumstance arises. This also applies to worship. If the Lord is our dearest "Loved One," then we should remain committed to Him in worship no matter what the circumstances or how it might make us look to others. That is manly worship. Spiritually committed men are not afraid to worship the Lord when others are watching.

5. "I don't want to be a hypocrite." What we are really saying here is, *People may think that I am not real in my worship so I will not worship at all.* Have you ever heard of a man at a football game not cheering for his team that just scored because he didn't want to be hypocritical? Of course not. So why we do we hesitate to worship the Lord for fear someone may think we are hypocrites? Must we be perfect before we can worship the Lord? No. Many of us men want to look as if we are perfect; however, we will never know the grace of God until we acknowledge our weaknesses and handicaps. Then, as we see our faults in the light of His perfectness, we are repentant. Then is the best time to worship the Lord.

We can only show God's grace to others if we have

experienced it ourselves. God chose us knowing all the mistakes we would make and the many times we would let Him and our families down. Yet He had no second thoughts about calling us. His love for us is very great, and we do not have to be perfect to express our love to Him. Real men are secure enough in their relationship with the Lord to be transparent in their worship of Him.

Can men really worship the Lord as the woman at Simon's house did? Jesus did not discourage the woman's overflow of emotion. I believe that Jesus was saying to us that this kind of extravagant expression has a place in our worship life. Because she was forgiven many things she loved Him greatly, and she expressed that love outwardly in lavish veneration. I believe Jesus expects men to do the same.

Some would call this kind of worship extreme. I used to think that this extravagant worship was more feminine than masculine. But "extreme" worship is relative; it is dependent upon where each of us is. Because the woman was forgiven much, she worshiped much. To those who feel they have been forgiven little this may seem unnecessarily extreme. Who determines what is too far, too extreme? You and I, or Jesus?

When we worship with lavishness it is not a waste of time, energy, or expression. Our worship, however extreme or extravagant, is for the Lord and His eyes only. So many of us men want to say, "Pardon my lack of worship. I am a man, you see." But Jesus' encounters with the scribes and Pharisees and His teachings about those who hesitate with various excuses show that He does not exempt anyone from showing devotion to Him. Our first obligation to our Creator is passionate worship, and we are not excused from this commandment because we are men or for any other reason.

■ ■ ■ ■ ■

FIVE

The God We Worship

Two thousand women gathered in Minneapolis in November 1993 for an event called "ReImaging." Conference attenders examined pantheistic religions and the heretical gnostic gospels to "reimagine" a new god and a new means to salvation. Sophia is the embodiment of wisdom, found in the first nine chapters of Proverbs, they claimed. The women thanked, blessed, and praised Sophia as their deity.

What makes this phenomenon unique is that these women were from the United Methodist Church (UMC), the Presbyterian Church U.S.A., the Evangelical Lutheran Church in America, and the American Baptist Church. Supposedly, they were Christians. Clergy attended the event as well. The ReImaging conference was held in connection with the World Council of Churches' Decade of Churches in Solidarity and was called by some "the Second Awakening."

This unorthodox feminist worship and teaching outraged several retired United Methodist bishops, who declared, "No comparable heresy has appeared in the church in the last fifteen centuries."[1] The head of the Women's Division of the UMC defended their participation, saying those "who attended this event are all mature women able to make discriminating theological judgments."[2] Ecumenical Church Women United affirmed "the absolute right of women to develop theological understandings rooted in their own realities and experiences."[3]

In keeping with their feminist theology, many of the thirty-four speakers accused the church of causing oppression of women, violence in the streets, child abuse, racism, classism, sexism, and even pollution. They charged this was due to the patriarchal (rule by father) construction of the church. Sophia, the women said, was with God at the creation, and she is "the tree of life to those who lay hold of her."[4]

"Sophia, we celebrate the nourishment of your milk and honey," the women toasted at a banquet table of creation that replaced the Lord's Supper. Several images were created and celebrated at the event that was planned by women leaders from mainline denominations of the Christian church.[5]

This conference in Minneapolis is one example of this generation's move to emasculate God, or to make Him more feminine. Why would people want to do this? Could it be because some people hate the behaviors they are seeing in the masculine gender? Men have given them some very good reasons to hate us—adultery, incest, child abuse, wife abuse, to name just a few.

In this generation, more and more men and women are living dysfunctional lives. This has both caused and resulted in the deterioration in the quality of family life.

Children who have been the victims of their parents' sins develop hatred toward their parents. They are bitter toward them for splitting up their family, for their abusiveness, for adultery, or for drug abuse. These children often grow up to be bitter toward all authority figures. They often hate God because of their parents' behavior. A child's father is meant to be the image of God to him on earth. Today with the demise of the father's integral role as the masculine, strength-giving head of the family, that image is under attack. God as our Heavenly Father is being ridiculed, denied, and destroyed.

But no matter how distorted the "fatherhood" of God's nature becomes, we cannot separate masculinity from God. The truth of what God is remains constant whether we believe it or not. What the Bible declares Him to be, is Who He is. Even if the entire world were atheists, or worshiped another God, it wouldn't change His nature or His attributes. Our heavenly Father, as He is revealed in the Bible, is immutable, unchangeable. God said of Himself, "I change not!" (Mal 3:6). We believe in God *the Father* and in *the man,* Jesus, as His eternal Son, not because we choose it to be that way, but because that is the way God has revealed Himself to us.

THE NEW SHE-BIBLE

The Inclusive Language Electionary Committee of the National Council of Churches is attempting to create nonsexist language about God. Their "edition" of the

Bible changes the phrase "God the Father" to "God the Father and Mother." But based on what the Bible tells us, when we feminize God, we deceive ourselves and distort our own understanding.

People feminize God because we want God to be loving, forgiving, and merciful. We want Him to *mother* us. We have legitimate needs. We need to be loved, and we need to be forgiven. We need to have mercy and grace extended to us. God does indeed have the nature and characteristics of a mother. He is merciful, caring, comforting, loving, and patient. Aren't we glad God is like that! However, when we feminize God in the image of our mother, it removes much of His masculine character.

People love the merciful, loving part of God's nature. But some dislike the God who is a holy, righteous judge; Law-giver and King; a God who requires obedience and pronounces judgment on the wicked. Those who try to delete the masculine characteristics of God are wanting to ignore these attributes of His divine nature.

We tend to view God through the same lenses as we viewed our parents, and often we attribute the characteristics of our strongest parent to Him. If Dad was not "present" in the home—even though his *body* may have been there—and our mother was our dominant parent to us, then God may be more like our mother to us. If our father was a strong presence in our lives and we liked our father, then God may look like our father. If we didn't like or respect our father, it may be hard to worship our Father Who is in heaven. But feminizing God or distorting His real image in any way affects our worship. When we lower Him to our point of need, we lower our worship of Him.

MALE AND FEMALE CHARACTERISTICS
IN THE NATURE OF GOD

In heaven the cry of mighty cherubs is "Holy, Holy, Holy." This is a strong declaration of God's complete uniqueness, because no other creature is worthy to be partners with Him in His excellency. Where do you find any other attribute of God trumpeted in praise like this? Is there any other song where a characteristic of God's nature is repeated three times? God is not just holy but infinitely holy. Holy in the highest possible degree. "Who among the gods is like you, O LORD? Who is like you—majestic in holiness, awesome in glory, working wonders?" (Ex 15:11, NIV). There is a throne in heaven with a Father ruling, and those that strive in the battle of sin can sit there with Him. A "mother-queen" does not sit there—a "Father-king" does.

This does not diminish the role of mothers or the motherly aspects of God. God is loving, merciful, and nurturing. Both men and women have these characteristics, but they are more associated with mothers. Jesus Himself referred to His ability to "mother" when He said to the Pharisees:

Jerusalem, Jerusalem, who kills the prophets and stones those who are sent to her! How often I wanted to gather your children together, the way a hen gathers her chicks under her wings, and you were unwilling.

MATTHEW 23:37, NASB

This passage clearly shows us that one of the motherly aspects of God's nature is that of nurturing and caring for His children. Similarly, Paul speaks of the character of his ministry by saying, "But we proved to be gentle among you, as a nursing mother tenderly cares for her own children" (1 Thes 2:7, NASB). The aspects of God's nature that are more associated with women are important characteristics of the nature of God and the attitude of Christian ministry. The point is, however, that those who try to feminize God would have a God who would eternally dote over us. This is a "me-centered" type of worship. Many of us flock to the kinds of Christian events that focus the primary attention on ourselves. People are, indeed, needy and require special attention. That is the role of the pastoral care ministry. However, if our worship is self-centered, it cannot be transcendent and God-focused.

Our worship should be motivated purely by our knowledge of Who God is. Such attributes as omnipotence, dominion, holiness, infinity, and immutability are those parts of God's character that cause our worship to rise up above the carnal realm of our own problems. True worship is worship that does not exalt Him for what He has done for us but for Who He is.

WORSHIP THE FATHER

Much about the Godhead is spoken of in male-gender terms. The Word became flesh to dwell among us as man.

As a newborn child, Jesus represented the mighty God to us. "For unto us a child is born, unto us a son is given: and the government shall be upon his shoulder: and his name shall be called Wonderful, Counseller, The mighty God, The everlasting Father, The Prince of Peace" (Is 9:6, KJV). This verse tells us that the everlasting Father has become a Son given. Such was His condescension in taking our nature upon Him; so did He humble and empty Himself in order to exalt and fill us. He is born into our world as a male child.

God has chosen to reveal Himself to humankind as a patriarch, or the father of a tribe or family. Jehovah was the Father of the nation of Israel. He formed the Israelites as a people and gave them their spiritual values and form of worship. They were a patriarchal society, in which the father governed the home and taught the family spiritual things. This was God's doing, and it was His desire that men be the spiritual leaders.

The Lord has disclosed Himself to us as Father of all creation. His relationship with us is more in the sense of a father than anything else. He is God our Father (see Romans 1:7). All things began with Him, and all things end with Him. "Then the end will come, when he hands over the kingdom to God the Father after he has destroyed all dominion, authority and power. For he must reign until he has put all his enemies under his feet" (1 Cor 15:24-25, NIV). That is a very masculine act.

One reason God sent His Spirit into our hearts at the time of our salvation is to solidify our relationship to Him as His sons and daughters. We are to call God "Father."

"Because you are sons, God sent the Spirit of his Son into our hearts, the Spirit who calls out, 'Abba, Father'" (Gal 4:6, NIV). Jesus taught us to pray:

> Our Father in heaven, hallowed be your name, your kingdom come, your will be done on earth as it is in heaven.... For if you forgive men when they sin against you, your heavenly Father will also forgive you. But if you do not forgive men their sins, your Father will not forgive your sins.
>
> MATTHEW 6:9-10, 14-15, NIV

Jesus revealed Creator-God as a "Father." He worshiped in prayer or praise by addressing His Father in this way:

> I praise you, Father, Lord of heaven and earth, because you have hidden these things from the wise and learned, and revealed them to little children. Yes, Father, for this was your good pleasure. All things have been committed to me by my Father. No one knows the Son except the Father, and no one knows the Father except the Son and those to whom the Son chooses to reveal him.
>
> MATTHEW 11:25-27, NIV

The God of the Bible is called the "Father of lights" (Jas 1:17), "God the Father" (Jn 16:28), "heavenly Father" (Mt 6:14), "Abba Father" (Mk 14:36), "Holy

Father" (Jn 17:11), "righteous Father" (Jn 17:25), "Father of mercies" (2 Cor 1:3), "Father of glory" (Eph 1:17), and "God and Father of our Lord Jesus Christ" (2 Cor 11:31). Jesus by the Holy Spirit taught us to worship the male-gender aspects of God. "But when you pray, go into your room, close the door and pray to your Father, who is unseen. Then your Father, who sees what is done in secret, will reward you" (Mt 6:6, NIV).

In the Psalms, David often spoke of God in male-gender terms. "Sing to God, sing praises to His name; cast up a highway for Him who rides through the deserts, whose name is the LORD, and exult before Him. A father of the fatherless and a judge for the widows is God in His holy habitation" (Ps 68:4-5, NASB). Paul also taught us to worship the Father in song. "Speaking to one another in psalms and hymns and spiritual songs, singing and making melody with your heart to the Lord; always giving thanks for all things in the name of our Lord Jesus Christ to God, *even the Father*" (Eph 5:19-20, NASB, emphasis mine).

Throughout the Bible, the "fatherhood" of God in relation to us, His children, is emphasized. God cannot be separated from His masculine attributes, and they are an important dimension of His spiritual headship in our lives. In the same way, we, as men, are to model this fatherhood and take on the leadership of our own families here on earth. By taking our appropriate masculine roles in our families we can reflect to our children the true image of our Heavenly Father. "In the same way, let your light shine before men, that they may see your good deeds and praise your Father in heaven" (Mt 5:16, NIV). And in so doing, our life itself will become an act of worship to the Father.

■ ■ ■ ■ ■

SIX

Intimacy with God

I was sitting in front of the television one day, channel surfing. I came across a bodybuilding contest. I would like to have a little more tone and bulk in my chest and arms, so I watched awhile. Someone was striking a pose showing clearly defined triceps, biceps, pectorals, and abdominals. I was quite impressed by the person's muscle definition. It wasn't long before I realized the bodybuilder was a woman.

Something is wrong with this picture, I thought to myself. She had all the bulk and shape of a man. She was so muscular that she had almost lost her feminine features; her figure lacked the soft curves most adult women possess. Why did she want to look like that? Perhaps she found it attractive or just wanted to push herself to the limits of body building. Whatever it was that motivated this woman, she had developed so many masculine characteristics that she lost her feminine attractiveness. She had all the components that would make a woman attractive, but she was not. Why? She had lost touch with her own identity.

I couldn't help but compare her to the church—the bride of Christ. Has the bride of Christ lost its own identity, its sense of purpose and calling? Have we as a church lost our softness, our responsiveness to Christ, and replaced it with "machismo"?

EXTREME MALENESS

"Machismo" (or "macho") is the exaggerated expression of masculinity. It pushes the definition of manhood to the outer edge of the manliness continuum where it becomes a weird, alien, or deformed image. The same principle applies to the church. When we, as the bride of Christ, are overly masculine, we rob the church of her God-given softness and attractiveness, causing her to appear as a woman bodybuilder.

In one parable, Jesus describes the kingdom of heaven using a feminine analogy. He says the kingdom of heaven is like ten virgins eager to meet the bridegroom.

Five of them were foolish and five were wise. The foolish ones took their lamps but did not take any oil with them. The wise, however, took oil in jars along with their lamps. The bridegroom was a long time in coming, and they all became drowsy and fell asleep. At midnight the cry rang out: "Here's the bridegroom! Come out to meet him!" Then all the virgins woke up and trimmed their lamps. The foolish ones said to the wise, "Give us some of your oil; our lamps are going out." "No," they replied, "there may not be enough for both us and you. Instead, go to those who sell oil and buy some for yourselves." But while they were on their way to buy the oil, the bridegroom arrived. The virgins who were ready went in with him to the wedding banquet. And the door was shut. Later the others also came. "Sir! Sir!" they said. "Open the door for us!" But he replied, "I tell you the truth, I don't know you." Therefore keep watch, because you do not know the day or the hour.

MATTHEW 25:2-13, NIV

As a church, we are to prepare for that marriage banquet as these women prepared.

Until these virgins heard the cry that the bridegroom was coming, they would wait and watch. So we are to be attendants to Christ, honoring Him with our lives and our worship, longing for our Husband as a bride-in-waiting. "I will betroth you to me forever; I will betroth you in righteousness and justice, in love and compassion" (Hos 2:19, NIV).

The function of the church is to be a bride of our Lord—to love and respond to His headship as a woman would respond to her husband, to honor and revere Him, to lovingly serve Him. The church as the bride is also to respond to the love of her Husband in worship. This is the center of our relationship with Him. It is what gives our relationship depth and meaning because worship is our communication, our interaction and life-flow with Christ. The destiny of the church is to be united with our Husband for eternity. Our eternal relationship with Him will be as a husband and wife. We must guard against the extreme masculinity or "machismo" that would keep us from responding to Him.

SONS WHO ARE A BRIDE

There is an intimacy in our interaction with our bridegroom that may seem too feminine for some men. As men, we follow Christ as sons, soldiers, athletes, and servants. He is our captain, our teacher, and our Savior. Inasmuch, He is also our husband. Our inability as men to see ourselves as warriors, conquerors, and kings who are also the bride of Christ is the reason why many men in the church are hung up about passionate worship. We are too much like the Marlboro Man—dirty, tough, independent, and passionless.

It's hard for the Marlboro men types to worship, not because they are so manly but because they are so insecure about what others think. They feel it is important to be strict, cold, stable, unmovable, and silent to prove to everyone they are not emotional or passionate. They do not want to appear as an anxious young bride.

Understanding how to be the bride of Christ means cultivating intimacy and closeness to Jesus Christ. God wants to be close to those who have given their lives to Him. "He is intimate with the upright" (Prv 3:32). Jesus told Martha, the sister of Mary, that only one thing is necessary (see Luke 10:42), and that one thing is intimacy with Him.

As Jesus and his disciples were on their way, he came to a village where a woman named Martha opened her home to him. She had a sister called Mary, who sat at the Lord's feet listening to what he said. But Martha was distracted by all the preparations that had to be made. She came to him and asked, "Lord, don't you care that my sister has left me to do the work by myself? Tell her to help me!" "Martha, Martha," the Lord answered, "you are worried and upset about many things, but only one thing is needed. Mary has chosen what is better, and it will not be taken away from her."

LUKE 10:38-42, NIV

As believers we have a responsibility to draw close to our Savior. This can be done in prayer, praise, reading of the Word, and the Lord's Supper. All of it, however, is worship. These spiritual disciplines are not ends in themselves. Rather, they are avenues for us to draw near to the Lord.

Intimacy comes before ministry or service to God. When we become more intimate with God, we acquire a touch of the Lord on our spirit, attitudes, and behavior. Each of those becomes more like Christ, and we have a greater perception of what the Lord's desires are, moment by moment. We cannot with much impact evangelize, teach, or witness prior to worship. If we are drawn to Him in worship, then we can run with Him in ministry.

INTIMACY AND ANXIETY

Mary and Martha lived in Bethany with their brother Lazarus. They provided for Jesus the nearest thing to a home.

The third year of Jesus' ministry was a year of opposition. He was two miles southeast of Jerusalem when He visited Mary and Martha. Within six months from this event Jesus would be crucified.

Don McMinn, a Southern Baptist minister and author from Dallas, Texas, makes some interesting points about intimacy.[1] He says, first of all, that intimacy is more important than our work and serving. Jesus said that "Mary has chosen what is better." Jesus considered serving Him to be a distraction from worshiping Him. Business and activity is the enemy to intimacy.

Secondly, intimacy involves a choice that must be made. We don't drift into intimacy. We have to make a choice to draw near. "Come near to God and he will come near to you" (Jas 4:8, NIV). Mary made a *choice* to draw near. Martha did not. It doesn't run in the family to be intimate with the Lord; it is a decision of the will, and each of us must make that personal decision. Mary made a different choice than Martha, and the Lord said it was the better choice.

Thirdly, intimacy is the antidote for anxiety. Jesus said to Martha, "Martha, you are worried and troubled about many things." Martha was fretting and fussing about her elaborate preparations. She had many cares and troubles. She was anxious. How often are we that way? So many things distract us from intimacy with the Lord. The seemingly urgent tends to crowd out the truly important.

Someone once said, "Anxiety is a mild case of atheism." When we worry about things we are making a confession of faith: "God is not able to take care of it." Christian men should not be anxious about their affairs.

> Be anxious for nothing, but in everything by prayer and supplication with thanksgiving let your request be made known to God. And the peace of God, which surpasses all comprehension, shall guard your hearts and your minds in Christ Jesus.
>
> PHILIPPIANS 4:6 NASB

Intimacy causes Jesus to seek us. God doesn't have "favorites" but "intimates." The Lord is looking for those who will worship Him, not mechanically or legalistically, but personally and intimately. The Father is seeking those who will worship Him in spirit and in truth.

WHEN INTIMACY IS ABSENT

Martha was trying to be in control, but her lack of intimacy was causing her to lose control. From Martha's behavior in this story, we can glean many lessons about what happens to us when intimacy with our Lord takes a backseat to our service or to other priorities in our lives.

Men who experience very little intimacy with the Lord often have a complaining spirit. Martha came from the kitchen area into the room where Jesus was and said, "Lord, don't you care?" Anyone who knows the Lord Jesus as their Savior knows that Jesus cares. But when we are busy and lacking intimacy with Christ, we do not think clearly. Our emotions and our spirits get out of control. Martha complained. Was it her guest's fault? Was Jesus the cause for Martha's anxiousness? Yet those who are lacking in their private worship with the Lord more easily fall into complaining. When we see that happening in our lives, we should run to the secret place and spend some intimate time with the Lord.

Those who lack intimacy with the Lord have only token reverence for authority. Martha rebuked the Lord when she said, "Lord, do you not care?" She challenged Jesus with her comment. Who is Martha to challenge the Lord? Who are you and I to complain to Him and challenge His ability to do things? It is His kingdom. He rules. When we haven't spent time with the Lord, our problems take precedent over our praise.

Those who lack intimacy with our Lord often become self-centered or selfish. Martha said, "My sister left me to do the work." The emphasis was on Martha. "My" sister left "me" to do all the preparations by "myself." Who asked her to make a meal anyway? Perhaps she wanted to bless and impress Jesus. In her eyes what she was doing was the most important thing. Her priorities were not Jesus' priorities for her. How often do we assume things need to be done? These are assumptions and presumptions. Did anyone ask Jesus what He wanted? Only one thing is necessary!

There was a time in my life when I got so caught up in what I thought I *had to do* that I became oblivious to the needs and desires of my family. My ministry had grown. The more I achieved, the more I wanted to achieve. The more projects I had going, the more important I seemed in my own eyes. I was driven by my desires and agendas. During this time I didn't spend much time with the Lord. I was too busy accomplishing very important things. After all, I was on a "mission for God." Funny, He had never given me those things to do. They were my ideas. Like Martha, I had presumed that it was what the Lord wanted.

By God's grace my pastor saw what was happening and confronted me about some behavior and attitudes. I had been deceived, thinking everything was okay, that things would just work themselves out. Everything was okay, but only in my own eyes.

"You must stop your ministry for awhile and concentrate on your personal life and family life, or you will destroy your marriage, family, and ministry altogether," my pastor advised me. I took some time off to get back in touch with what was really important. My pastor and friends helped me see how to be a better husband and father. I spent that time in prayer, talking with and loving my wife, hugging and playing with our sons. The deception that I had been under slowly began to disappear.

I began to see the "real" world and the "real" responsibilities God had called me to as a man.

Those six months were very hard for me, especially on my ego. I was embarrassed that I was spiritually handicapped. What would people think of me? They may think I am not perfect. No one is, yet I saw myself as perfect in my own eyes—the greatest and the best.

My wife and I went through counseling. We began to see areas in my life that were out of order, and I realized how deep my deception had become. I began to build my personal devotional life again. It is strange that I could teach about worship for more than fifteen years and have such a lack in my own private worship.

I thank God for that season in my life. I learned many important things about relationships. I discovered where I was weak and began, with the help of both my wife and my pastor, to draw borders and construct hedges in my life that would keep me safe from further deception. If it is at all possible, I would recommend that kind of sabbatical for every man. It helped me to wake up, to see my family as the greatest responsibility God has entrusted to me, and to put them above my work and ministry.

Men who are deficient in intimacy in worship will be demanding. "Tell her to help me." Martha made a demand on the Lord. When we go to the Lord supposedly in an intimate time of prayer, do we communicate to the Lord in a loving and submissive way, or do we demand that He fulfill our shopping list? This is not intimacy at all. It may have the appearance of a pious man who is always in prayer, but making petitions of the Lord is not necessarily intimate worship. We must check our own hearts and attitude when we go to the Lord in prayer.

Men who are deficient in intimacy will concentrate on things instead of relationships. How true this is. I wrestle with this as much as most men. I love having toys— mobile phones, radar detectors, notebook computers, portable CD players, VCRs, TVs, video cameras, new cars, etc. But the more things we have, the more they demand our time. I have not had time to learn all that my new computer does, never mind my video camera or mobile phone. I know enough only to do some of the things that are possible on each one. I don't have enough time to explore my toys to their fullest potential. When will I ever have time to surf the Internet?

With the explosion of technology, there will be more and more toys that we just *have* to have. If we think we don't have enough time now to worship the Lord, then we certainly won't in the future. We must, as men, make a commitment to intimate worship with the Lord. It is a discipline that will shape our lives. When we get to the secret place, we will realize that this is more fun than playing with any of the toys we own. We will realize more and more that we were built for relationship with God, and not simply to acquire *things*.

PRACTICAL INTIMACY

James Robison once said, "Ministry must flow from an intimate relationship with the Lord. There is no substitute for time spent with Him.... Through intimacy with God I've learned that the greatest in the kingdom is truly the servant of others."[2]

David Yonggi Cho, pastor of a 750,000-member church, is very disciplined about his time with the Lord. "I'm not smart enough to solve the thousands of problems that come to me regularly. Yet I can say to the Holy Spirit: 'Sweet Spirit, please let me tell You about the problem I have. I know You know the mind of God and You already have the answer.' With assurance, I then await the answer from the Holy Spirit. Through these many years I have discovered that the Holy Spirit renews me spiritually, mentally, and physically. I have seen that daily communion with the Holy Spirit is a necessity. Out of the one hour that I spend in prayer every morning, much of that time is spent in fellowship with the Holy Spirit."[3]

I recommend that you make a daily appointment with the Lord. Write it on your calendar or "to-do" list. Don't leave it to chance. Put it on your schedule as a standing appointment. Make a commitment to meet Him at the same time and place every day. If you leave it to chance, it will not become a regular habit.

Most people find that spending time with God in the morning works best. If we leave it to the evening hours the day's schedule may back up and cheat us out of our prayer time. We may also spend more time giving God a damage report of the day instead of receiving fresh direction for the new day. The morning is also the quietest time of the day.

Early morning time with God seems to have been the habit of David and of Jesus. David said, "My voice shalt thou hear in the morning, O LORD; in the morning will I direct my prayer unto thee, and will look up" (Ps 5:3, KJV).

Jesus also sought private time with His Father in the early morning. After a full day in Capernaum teaching at the synagogue, delivering a man from demons, healing Simon's mother-in-law and many who were sick, and casting out many more demons, Jesus needed to spend time with His Father. So the next day before the sun was up, He went off to be with His Father. The Bible says, "Very early in the morning, while it was still dark, Jesus got up, left the house and went off to a solitary place, where he prayed" (Mk 1:35, NIV).

The Bible says when you pray, go into "your inner room, and when you have shut your door, pray to your Father who is in secret, and your Father who sees in secret will repay you" (Mt 6:6). There must be a private place in your home away from the distractions of life where you can pray. It is important to find a specific location to meet with God. It may be a certain room, a favorite chair, looking out a particular window, or on a patio. Wherever the location, it should be private. Shut the door. Perhaps you should take the phone out of the room permanently. Protect yourself from interruptions.

Then follow a strategy. Set an agenda that you want to follow. (This will keep you from daydreaming.) A simple and effective plan may be to divide the time into three equal parts—praise, reading Scripture, and prayer. Develop a pattern for what you want to accomplish with your time with God and do it every day.

During the praise time express to God your thankfulness for Who He is and not just what He has done for you. He is the Eternal One, Creator of all things, and the all-Powerful One. This time of praise can be strengthened by playing a worship tape softly in the background. The atmosphere of praise will deepen your experience with the Lord.

Read the Bible following a systematic pattern of reading. I personally enjoy following a schedule that helps me finish the Bible in twelve months. This will give you scriptures for each day. You might also read a chapter of the New Testament every day. Whatever you choose, be systematic.

During your prayer time make your requests known to God. I would encourage you to spend as much time listening to God as you do talking to Him. Prayer is a two-way conversation. Make a journal and write down what He tells you. Then be sure to act on it.

Enjoy your time with the Lord. Our time with God should be a pleasant and rewarding experience. Don't let it become burdensome and boring. Don't let your time feel like an obligation and something that you have to do. You are part of a love relationship, not a contractual agreement. Get in touch with your feminine side and, as a bride, build the romantic aspects of your relationship with your Bridegroom. If you miss a couple of mornings don't condemn yourself and hide from God the rest of the week. He is not that disturbed because you missed your time with Him. Jump right back into your habit the next morning. Your relationship with God as your Bridegroom is not that insecure. Jesus wants to provide daily bread for you and your loved ones. He wants to provide strength for you physically, emotionally, spiritually, and mentally. He will fill you and prepare you for the day and unfold to you your destiny day by day.

■   ■   ■   ■   ■

SEVEN

The Man as Servant-Leader

The hammer made a dull "thud" as it struck the long iron spike. It quickly pierced the prisoner's hand, pinning it to the wooden beam. When both hands were fastened securely, the soldier nailed the man's feet tightly to the wood.

"Let's lift it up," he commanded.

The soldiers hoisted the wooden frame and let it drop in the hole. There the man hung, above the ground, dripping blood from His pierced flesh.

"If you are the King of the Jews save yourself!" the soldiers mocked, throwing wine vinegar into His face.

One of the sentenced men who hung on a similar frame nearby hurled insults at Him: "Aren't you the Christ? Save yourself and us!"

He was rebuked by a fellow criminal saying, "Don't you fear God since you are under the same sentence? We are punished justly, for we are getting what our deeds deserve. But this man has done nothing wrong."

Then he said to the man hanging in the center, "Jesus, remember me when you come into your kingdom."

It was on Golgotha, the place of the skull, that Jesus

willingly gave His life. It was a painful and shameful death. He was reviled and reproached, and treated with scorn and contempt. The people stood beholding Him, not at all concerned but rather pleased with the spectacle. They criticized Him for the good works He had done. They triumphed over Him as if they had conquered Him, and they challenged Him to save Himself while He was in the very act of purchasing their salvation.

They knew that the Christ was the chosen of God. The Jewish rulers jeered Him as a false Messiah because He did not honor their hypocrisy nor did He fight the Romans as if His kingdom was of this world. The Roman soldiers mocked Him as the King of the Jews. They made sport with Him and made a jest of His sufferings.

Jesus was the example of a great man bearing responsibility for other people. Jesus took the burden of taking care of our sins. He did not wait to be asked. Jesus did what was required. It wasn't even for good people that He died. It was for all those that sinned against God. We didn't deserve His act of kindness. However, He did what was required that we might have eternal life. That is what great men do—take responsibility to do what is required of them.

Like Jesus, men are to bear responsibility for those that God has given them. Real men selflessly do what is required to help their families. They do what is right without waiting for them to ask for help and whether they deserve it or not.

QUITTING IS NOT AN OPTION

Mike worked with Joe Gibbs and his home for troubled youth called Youth For Tomorrow. He was determined not to be a quitter, despite many setbacks in his life, Mike persevered.

Mike was raised in a Christian home but had been in and out of numerous juvenile detention centers, including, at the age of fifteen, the state mental hospital. "Once when I was alone and penniless," Mike said, "I remember climbing into a trash dumpster at Pizza Hut to find other people's food which had been thrown away. That is when I came face-to-face with the thought of suicide. At midnight I called a friend. He agreed to come to my rescue. My response was, "Don't come here at 1:15 A.M., because it will be too late." Mike was determined to give up and take his life.

When the paramedics did find Mike he was close to death. They began beating his chest and yelling, "He's gone!" But a few minutes later they brought him back to life. Mike had another chance to live.

Mike had so many drug overdoses that the hospitals in northern Virginia knew him by his first name. He denied his addiction to alcohol and drugs. Despite his many faults and bad habits Mike became a success in the business world as a builder. Money excited him and led him to further addiction. His wife and children all suffered because of his lack of responsibility. Thinking only of himself, he put his desires for pleasure above the needs and desires of his family. Mike was unwilling to stop his self-indulgence for the sake of others. He felt no responsibility for them. Consequently, he lost his wife and his life began falling apart again.

Many times Mike made deals with God, much like his big-time drug deals, hoping God would spare his life one more time. Yet, each time he would go back to the old life. After a fluke building accident that damaged his eyes, the doctors said that Mike would not see again. However, God totally restored his sight. Another time an oak tree was blown over on the truck he was in. Again God spared his life.

After losing everything precious to him, Mike gave his life to Jesus Christ. What was left of his business he turned over to the Lord. Then the economy went bad, and his business began to fail. "But through it all, God has given me a message of hope," Mike declares in a motivational speech. "Quitting is not an option!" Real men do not walk off the football field and quit the team because they are behind. Real men take responsibility to see things through despite the difficulty that is ahead of them. Today Mike speaks to thousands of young people with a message of hope whether for Youth For Tomorrow near Washington, D.C., or Potomac High School, or Young Life rallies.

Ephesians 5 tells us not to run away from responsibility, but to take a proactive approach to loving our wives and caring for our families:

Husbands, love your wives, just as Christ also loved the church and gave Himself up for her. Husbands, love your wives, just as Christ loved the church, and gave Himself for it. So husbands ought also to love their own wives as their own bodies. He who loves his own wife loves himself.

EPHESIANS 5:25, 28, NASB

The Bible does *not* say to love our wives until they no longer thrills us. We are to love our wives like Christ loved the church. And the church was the harlot who was unfaithful to Him, and God loved her anyway. How much more are we to be faithful and steadfast to the promise and covenant we have made with our wives. We are to give our lives for our wives just as Christ did for us.

A real man will give his life for his family. We are not promised anything out of the deal. We are simply to take the responsibility. Jesus was not promised any benefits when He gave His life for us. He did it because He had been given responsibility for us.

THE BLAME GAME

It is easy to understand how men in our culture might be tempted to shirk our responsibilities. We live in a culture of irresponsibility. Everyone blames everyone else for their problems. The African-Americans blame the Caucasians. The Caucasians blame the African-Americans. The Hispanics blame the Koreans, and on and on it goes. The poor blame the rich for their poverty. The rich blame the poor for the condition they are in. Businesses blame their employees, and employees blame businesses. Most everyone blames someone else for their situations.

The eighties and nineties are the decades of lawsuits. McDonald's was sued by a woman who purchased a hot cup of coffee at their drive-in window and foolishly held it between her legs while she was driving. The coffee spilled and she was burned. Even our children have been told: "Coffee is hot. It will burn." But the woman filed a lawsuit against McDonald's and won. Individual rights have gone bizarre. We have become a nation of complainers.

We have also become a nation of "deadbeat dads," running from the responsibility of taking care of our children. Many men leave home because they are tired of paying the bills, tired of the responsibility. So they run from the pressure. They cop out on their families. The casualties are their wives and children. The man doesn't suffer as much as the innocent suffer.

Single mothers are the product of men's irresponsibility. Women who have been victimized begin to hate men, and they have reason to. We give them excuses to despise us. We give them reasons to think less of manhood.

But when things get very dark, as they are in our society today, a little light—even a single candle—shines brightly. In a society that is so irresponsible, showing a little responsibility is radical. Today, a husband and a father who is being conscientious and serving his family the best he can is radical.

A LOVING RESPONSIBILITY

Adam and Jesus are two men that represent all of us. When Adam fell we all fell. His sin affected all mankind, and he was responsible for the sinful nature we have received. When Christ died for us, He took responsibility to change the impact that sin had on us. When He rose from the dead, we all benefited from His action.

> For if, by the trespass of the one man, death reigned through that one man, how much more will those who receive God's abundant provision of grace and of the gift of righteousness reign in life through the one man, Jesus Christ. Consequently, just as the result of one trespass was condemnation for all men, so also the result of one act of righteousness was justification that brings life for all men. For just as through the disobedience of the one man the many were made sinners, so also through the obedience of the one man the many will be made righteous.
>
> ROMANS 5:17-19, NIV

"So it is written: 'The first man Adam became a living being; the last Adam, a life-giving spirit'" (1 Cor 15:45). The word *Adam* simply means "man." The first "man" became a living being; the last "man" became a life-giving spirit. The natural man came first, then the spiritual man. The first man was of the dust of the earth. The last man was from heaven. And just as we have borne the physical likeness of the earthly man, so shall we bear the spiritual likeness of the man from heaven. Ultimately, we will be like Jesus.

What does this mean for us now in this earthly life? Jesus took upon Himself the responsibility for every bad thing we have done. He didn't die just for good people. He died for bad people. He took our blame. Jesus did not say, "Look what you did! I am free from any obligation to help you." Instead, knowing all our sins, He took the burden of responsibility to do what was needed to make things right. The buck stopped with Him. He chose to cover us anyway and displayed the ultimate act of loving responsibility.

This is the way Christ wants us to love our wives and families. We are responsible to love our wives as Christ loved us. We must be willing to take the burden, the responsibility, for our wives' actions and attitudes.

Have we ever been guilty of defending ourselves by saying, "Well, look what she did to me!" "Do you know what she did?" But does the sin of the other exempt us from the responsibility to continue to do what is right? No. If the other person has done something wrong we are often too willing to cast blame and get out of our commitment to her. Who is perfect anyway? We can always find an excuse why we should not be responsible anymore.

The Lord tells a story of a man who didn't have to take responsibility but chose to.

A man was going down from Jerusalem to Jericho, when he fell into the hands of robbers. They stripped him of his clothes, beat him and went away, leaving him half dead. A priest happened to be going down the same road, and when he saw the man, he passed by on the other side. So too, a Levite, when he came to the place and saw him, passed by on the other side. But a Samaritan, as he traveled, came where the man was; and when he saw him, he took pity on him. He went to him and bandaged his wounds, pouring on oil and wine. Then he put the man on his own donkey, took him to an inn and took care of him. The next day he took out two silver coins and gave them to the innkeeper. "Look after him," he said, "and when I return, I will reimburse you for any extra expense you may have." Which of these three do you think was a neighbor to the man who fell into the hands of robbers? The expert in the law replied, "The one who had mercy on him." Jesus told him, "Go and do likewise."

LUKE 10:30-37, NIV

The Good Samaritan took responsibility for the man's condition and even put his resources on the line for the victim. "Whatever it takes, charge it to my account," he said. Sometimes the reason we run from responsibility is because we are afraid we will be consumed by responsibility for other people.

Prior to telling the story of the Good Samaritan, Jesus told about the two greatest commandments:

A rich young lawyer asked Jesus what he had to do to receive eternal life.

Jesus asked him, "What does the law say?"

The lawyer answered: "'Love the Lord your God with all your heart and with all your soul and with all your strength and with all your mind'; and, 'Love your neighbor as yourself.'"

"You have answered correctly," Jesus replied. "Do this and you will live."

But the lawyer did not want to be responsible for loving others so he asked Jesus, "Who is my neighbor?" The lawyer was hoping to get out of responsibility.

Although the rich young lawyer may fall short of our description of a great man, this story points out two characteristics of a man that are very important to Jesus. First, a real man worships God with his heart, soul, mind, and strength, and second, he does not run from responsibility for his neighbor but bears the burdens of those with whom he is in covenant.

TAKING THE LEAD

It's easy to be a Monday morning quarterback. When we become a spectator, we not only turn into a critic, but an expert critic. Men need to get off the couch and take an active role in the lives of their wives and children. Men are critical and sometimes irate about what goes on at the local school. But are we willing to get involved to make a difference?

Men are created by God to be leaders. Fathers are to teach their children about spiritual things. In the Bible children were to imitate their fathers. "Be imitators of God, copy Him *and* follow His example—as well-beloved children (imitate their father)" (Eph 5:1, AMP). They were to learn from their fathers' words and behavior. The father was a servant-teacher to his family. Men must lead in prayer, Scripture reading, worship, and in seeking God.

Fathers are to be servants, leaders, and priests of their home. In Deuteronomy 6, God told Moses to teach his children how to worship.

These are the commands, decrees and laws the LORD your God directed me to teach you to observe in the land that you are crossing the Jordan to possess, so that you, your children and their children after them may fear the LORD your God as long as you live by keeping all his decrees and commands that I give you, and so that you may enjoy long life.

DEUTERONOMY 6:1-3, NIV

Do you know that men are supposed to teach their grandsons about worship?

Hear, O Israel: The LORD our God, the LORD is one. Love the LORD your God with all your heart and with all your soul and with all your strength. These commandments that I give you today are to be upon your hearts. Impress them on your children. Talk about them when you sit at home and when you walk along the road, when you lie down and when you get up. Tie them as symbols on your hands and bind them on your foreheads. Write them on the door frames of your houses and on your gates.

DEUTERONOMY 6:4-9, NIV

Constantly remind your children to "love the Lord your God with all your heart, with all your soul, with all your might, and all your strength."

A man's role in worship is to be a priest to God and to his family. The biblical pattern of the family is that of government by the father. As the servant-leader, men need to step up to the plate and assume the responsibility of leadership. But to the same degree that they lead, they are to serve and lay down their lives for their families.

■ ■ ■ ■ ■

EIGHT

Leading Our Families

It is important for a man to understand how to be a great dad in the eyes of his kids. Most of us want an instruction manual, filled with all the practical "how-tos." But having one doesn't mean we would actually read it because, at the same time, we don't want anyone to tell us how to rear our children. Leading is something of a paradox, and since most men don't know where to begin, we do nothing. But our children desperately need our leadership and our involvement in their lives. "Just Do It!" the Nike tennis shoe commercial says. That's where men need to be with their children—on the field "doing it" and not watching their lives from a seat on the sidelines. To be great in our children's eyes, we have to get involved.

First and foremost, men should take leadership in our children's spiritual lives. Are our wives having to say to us, "Let's read the Bible after supper"? Going along is better than not doing anything, but simply giving her the okay is not taking the lead. The kids need to see Dad taking the initiative. We must be the ones to instigate communication about spiritual principles. We must be the ones to instill wisdom in our children and to cause them to grow spiritually. We must share with them the secrets of life we have discovered. This is what will leave an impact on their lives.

Stephen Covey and Roger and Rebecca Merrill in their book, *First Things First*, say, "The key to the fire within is our spiritual need to leave a legacy.... By teaching our children principles instead of practices, or teaching them the principles behind the practices, we better prepare them to handle the unknown challenges of the future."[1]

Our involvement with our children now will enable them to make wise decisions for themselves when they grow up. It will also leave them a rich legacy of strong, powerful memories that will guide them through their lives, though we may no longer be with them. Such a legacy goes beyond our immediate family and touches our grandchildren and our great-grandchildren. The words that we speak today will outlive us, and the power of those words will touch even our descendants.

I heard a man recount how his grandfather impacted his life. His granddad showed interest in him and in the things he liked. He bought him a bike, and regularly they would take rides, stopping periodically to talk. The man can't remember much about the bike, but he remembers the wisdom his grandfather shared with him about life, about relationships, and about God. What he said had an unforgettable impact on the young boy's life into his manhood. What potential we have as men to leave a legacy for our children and grandchildren!

Often it seems easier to take the role of a leader in public than in the home. We want to look good in the eyes of those who don't even know us, and we go to great lengths to leave an impression on those in the community, on the job, and at church. In these places we are quick to rise up and lead. It is much harder to be a leader in our home, but that is where there is the greatest need.

WE DON'T HAVE TO BE PERFECT

There are a number of reasons why many men struggle with taking the lead in our homes. Perhaps we are plagued with low self-esteem, insecurity, and the fear of being viewed as hypocritical. We know that our family is aware of our weaknesses. They have seen us at our worst moments. Our private sins scream, "Failure!" in our faces, telling us we are disqualified to lead. We condemn ourselves, imagining what others might think. Our insecurity becomes a ball and chain that make us passive in our interaction with our loved ones.

However, effective leaders are not necessarily perfect men. "All have sinned," God says (Rom 3:23, NIV). "If we claim we have not sinned, we make him out to be a liar and his word has no place in our lives" (1 Jn 1:10, NIV). However, "if we confess our sins, he is faithful and just and will forgive us our sins and purify us from all unrighteousness" (1 Jn 1:9, NIV). Letting those who follow us see how we deal with our failures is a far greater help to them than trying to present a facade of perfection. It is a lie and deception to pretend to be something we are not. In Christ, there is grace and forgiveness for what has transpired in our families—even up to this very moment. We simply go to Him for cleansing when we falter. We cannot let our weaknesses and our pride keep us from taking our place as family leaders.

Neither can we allow our failures and weakness to hinder our relationship with God. When we feel we have failed in our leadership role and in God's eyes, it is sometimes difficult to maintain our close relationship with Him. But how do we get it right? Again, we must be willing to be transparent.

As a case in point, let's look at a scene that occurs in thousands of homes every Sunday. The family is getting ready to go to church, and the man wants to be on time. His wife is a little behind schedule, and he is getting upset. They arrive at church after the worship has already begun. Now they stand before God, but the husband is feeling ashamed about his attitude and does not want to get too close to the Lord. He keeps his distance and does not participate in the worship, except to sing along halfheartedly.

Because this man believes he has failed, he is not able to worship freely. He feels there is a barrier between God and him. Likewise, when we fail in our leadership roles, it may be difficult for us to worship. The key to warm, wholehearted worship is being in right standing with the Lord and others. How then can we come before God in worship when we have failed in our families? The answer is to clear up the blocks between us and the Lord by asking for forgiveness of attitudes and actions that are not right. After receiving God's forgiveness, there will be a clearness in our spirits that gives us a freshness and newness in our relationship with Him.

Real spirituality does not start with moral perfection. God doesn't require that we jump through hoops before we can have a relationship with Him. Friendship with God begins by coming to Him regularly for forgiveness. God doesn't keep a scorecard with all our failures listed. When we ask Him for forgiveness He declares us to be clean. God focuses on our relationship with Him, not on how perfect we are.

THE SHOW-OFF AND THE SINNER

Making mistakes does not disqualify us from leading our families. In fact, blowing it once in awhile and seeing our own weaknesses may help us depend more on God to do the job well. Some men have a lot of confidence in themselves and a high opinion of their own righteousness. They trust in their own good works as qualifying them as righteous. But Jesus had a parable to tell about men like these, a story about a Pharisee and a Publican.

Two men went up to the temple to pray, one a Pharisee and the other a tax collector. The Pharisee stood up and prayed about himself: "God, I thank you that I am not like other men—robbers, evildoers, adulterers—or even like this tax collector. I fast twice a week and give a tenth of all I get." But the tax collector stood at a distance. He would not even look up to heaven, but beat his breast and said, "God, have mercy on me, a sinner." I tell you that this man,

rather than the other, went home justified before
God. For everyone who exalts himself will be humbled, and he who humbles himself will be exalted.

LUKE 18:10-14, NIV

In this parable, Jesus contrasted the man who proudly
justified himself and the tax collector who humbly condemned himself. The Pharisee went to the temple to pray
because it was a public place, and there would be more
eyes on him. Most of the Pharisees were motivated by the
approval of men. Like the Pharisees, some men today keep
up the external performances of religion only to gain credit or to make themselves look good.

The Publican, on the other hand, went to the temple
because it was appointed to be a house of prayer for all
people. The Publican went to do his business with God
and to make his request known to God. God sees how we
come to Him and will judge us accordingly.

The Pharisee was so full of himself and his own goodness he did not feel a need for God's grace and favor. He
brought attention to himself because he was proud of his
position and accomplishments.

The Publican felt like a failure in spiritual terms. He was
broken, repentant, and he yearned for God. He expressed
his repentance and humility in his gesture. He kept at a
distance, sensing his unworthiness to draw near to God
and, perhaps, for fear of offending the Pharisee. The
Publican would not lift up his eyes to heaven, much less
his hands, as was usual in prayer. He had little confidence
and courage. But he did lift up his heart to God in the

heavens. His dejected appearance indicated his rejection of his own sin. The Publican smote his chest and prayed. Full of fear and shame, he made supplication for the mercy and grace of God.

Try as we might, we cannot establish our righteousness through our own efforts, as the Pharisees tried to do. No matter how much we worry about how our family will view us, we will never be free of making mistakes. The right action for us to take when we fall is that of the Publican: simply to humble ourselves, die to our pride, and call upon God for His mercy and grace.

In God's eyes there is not that much difference between the best of us and the worst of us. When a man is truly self-assured, it is because he has learned to trust in God's grace. Our confidence and success as priests in our homes will depend on our ability to trust the Lord to help us.

Remember the apostle Peter. When he denied Christ, he became a fallen leader, if only in his own eyes. He had blown it, and when he realized it, he went away, defeated and sorrowful. Everyone knew Peter had denied Christ, but Jesus did not think less of Peter. We know this because when Jesus rose from the dead, He sent the disciples to tell the brothers and Peter. Jesus had known then that Peter would blow it, and everyone would eventually know it too. Yet Peter is the one whom Jesus called 'the rock,' the one on whom He would build His church.

GETTING UP FROM A FALL

A friend of mine, a young minister, had an affair with a woman he had met. They saw each other a couple times. This had never happened to him before, and he tried to cut it off on the first meeting. But he met with the woman again.

He was disappointed in himself and devastated by the reality of what he had done. He worked hard to keep it a secret. He didn't want his wife and friends to know about his failure. The young man received much of his self-esteem from his performance as a minister and his spiritual service to others. Now, in his eyes, he was disqualified not only as a minister, but as a husband and father. He thought that there would be no way out of this. His family, his church, his friends, his community, and his ministry would be scandalized. He believed the lie that was whispered in his ear, "You have blown it forever. You will lose everything and never amount to anything." My friend had made a mistake, repented, and wanted to never do it again. But he had not experienced grace.

He did not know that, though it greatly hurt his wife, she would forgive him and help him through the situation. His pastor and friends who knew about the situation confronted him, counseled him, and forgave him. He realized that people are not as condemning as he had imagined them to be. When we confess our weakness, it lets people know that we are vulnerable like everyone else. Others are drawn to us because they can identify with what we have gone through. They too have weakness.

As a man you may ask, "How am I going to lead those that I have deeply hurt?" The answer is simple but requires much strength. Tell them you have wronged them and that you are very sorry. Ask for their forgiveness. They may, or may not, give it to you at that moment. But hang in there and begin to become the spiritual leader, and their forgiveness will eventually come.

How does this relate to worship? The Lord says, "If you are offering your gift at the altar and there remember that your brother has something against you, leave your gift there in front of the altar. First go and be reconciled to your brother; then come and offer your gift" (Mt 5:23-24, NIV). Some people cannot worship because they have such offense toward others and others toward them. One thing that sets us free to worship is being reconciled with those we love. We must take responsibility for what we have done. Ask forgiveness in an attitude of humility. This shows true spiritual leadership—not pretending nothing is wrong with you. Spiritual leadership is not a statement of spiritual maturity but responsibility. We lead not because we are more spiritually mature than anyone else, but because that is the function God has given us.

The Scriptures say, "The law was added so that the trespass might increase. But where sin increased, grace increased all the more" (Rom 5:20, NIV). When we are going through great difficulty, grace increases for us even more. The Lord is there and will help by arranging opportunities for repentance and putting people in our lives to reach out to us. If we do get up, we can go on, no less of a man, but a very real man.

A MAN'S PARISH

A man's home is his parish. It is his *church*, not his *castle*. Men are spiritually responsible before God for those who live in their household. The father is the priest of the home. In the Bible, priests have two primary functions. The first is to enter God's presence with sacrifices; the second is to stand in His presence on behalf of the needs of others. Like priests in a liturgical church, who are also called "fathers," men are to fill both roles for their families. The father stands before God on behalf of his family to intercede for them, and he brings their needs to the Father of heaven.

The Scriptures say, "I looked for a man among them who would build up the wall and stand before me in the gap" (Ez 22:30, NIV). In this passage, God states through Ezekiel that He was searching for an intercessor, one who could "fill the hole," but He found none. Sin makes a gap in the hedge of protection that surrounds a family. God wants men to stand in the gap, to cover their families in prayer, to make up the breach caused by sin and the works of the enemy. Men can do this by repentance, prayer, and reformation. God expects us to intercede and pray for our families. He wants to show mercy, to forgive and heal.

I make intercession for my family a regular part of my worship time with the Lord. Praying for the spiritual and physical health of my wife and sons is my responsibility as a priest of the home. If sickness attacks my sons or wife I go on the offensive to pray for their healing. If the family finances are out of sorts, I take it as my responsibility to intercede to God about them, not just hope next month is better. The effectual fervent prayer of a Christian man accomplishes much (Jas 5:16).

A father is the priest of his home, the home is his chapel, and his family is his congregation. We worship the Lord on behalf of our family, and we stand before Him for the needs of our family. Intercession for our wives and children is part of the function of a father.

The "man of the house" is the "minister of the house." He is the servant that represents God to the family and represents the family to God. He communicates the thoughts and ways of God to the family and brings them into an understanding of the invisible kingdom of God. Being the leader and priest in our families does not mean we have to be perfect. It simply means we accept the function that God has given us, and we depend upon His grace to do it well.

■ ■ ■ ■ ■

NINE

The Corporate Leader

"What am I doing here?" the smooth-skinned executive said to himself as he walked slowly through the bleak wasteland. His expensive clothes were dirty and torn from the journey that he was forced to take.

"I deserve better than this," he complained. "Where am I going?"

Out of the corner of his eye he saw a large snake slithering out of his way. He had been walking for many days now and had become used to the creatures of the desert. "All my training and experience must be worth something to somebody," he speculated. "There must have been some reason my life was miraculously spared when I was an infant."

He had been trained in the best schools in the nation. His grades in science, management, bookkeeping, law, and music were excellent. He had been groomed to be a leader of the largest and most powerful corporation in the world. Just when he was showing great promise and was about to be promoted to corporate executive, he was fired.

"I shouldn't have let my anger get out of hand," he

confessed. "That man might still be alive, and I wouldn't be in this mess." The boss had planned to get rid of him. So he had gone out to the desert, fleeing the murder charge.

This man felt he had failed miserably. All of his training and potential seemed so wasted. His future was uncertain, and it seemed it would be very short out in this dry land. He had found a tribe of wandering shepherds who took him in and gave him a job herding sheep.

One day when he was out in the desert pondering his future, a deep voice boomed across the desert, *"Moses!"* He was very startled, and stopped in his tracks. He quickly scanned the horizon to see where the voice came from.

Out in the distance there was a fire, and he ran over to see what was burning. He heard the voice again. "Moses!" This time it came from a burning, thorny shrub.

"I'm here," Moses answered cautiously.

The voice proceeded to tell him of his unique mission. This disillusioned leader was about to lead a nation of millions of slaves to forge a new country with its own economic, political, and religious systems. "I don't know if I'm up to this!" he thought to himself as the voice in the fire unfolded his future.

NOT ME!

Moses was a Levite. His father was Amran. When Moses was born, he was no ordinary child. He lived with his family only three months and then was adopted by

Pharaoh's daughter. Raised as her son, Moses was very knowledgeable and received the best education in all of Egypt. He was a man of powerful words and impressive action.

Loyal to his race, he defended a Hebrew slave who was being beaten by an Egyptian. With the great strength he possessed, Moses killed the Egyptian. Afterwards, he had to flee from Pharaoh to the desert of Midian.

Moses was eighty years old when he discovered the destiny for which he had been born and equipped. His discovery came in the midst of a season of disillusionment and failure. A man of education and potential, he was caring for farm animals. Moses, however, did not turn to wicked vices to feed his self-pity. He humbled himself and did what was required. It was in these circumstances that he received a call from God.

It is when we are faithfully conducting our business and are alone with God that we are in the best position to hear from Him. Righteous men who worship hear from the Lord. When Moses turned aside from his routine to seek the Lord, he received direction. Those who diligently seek God will find Him a rewarder. When we approach the Lord, He draws near to us. Moses learned more about God in the desert than in the palace of Pharaoh. God chooses the lowly and despised (Moses, now a shepherd) to put to shame the wise and strong (Pharaoh). Listen as God speaks to Moses:

"And now the cry of the Israelites has reached me, and I have seen the way the Egyptians are oppressing

them. So now, go. I am sending you to Pharaoh to
bring my people the Israelites out of Egypt." But
Moses said to God, "Who am I, that I should go to
Pharaoh and bring the Israelites out of Egypt?
Suppose I go to the Israelites and say to them, 'The
God of your fathers has sent me to you,' and they ask
me, 'What is his name?' Then what shall I tell them?"
God said to Moses, "I AM WHO I AM. This is what
you are to say to the Israelites: 'I AM has sent me to
you.'"

Exodus 3:9-11, 13-14, NIV

Moses objected to God calling him to deliver the
Hebrews from Egypt. He thought he was unworthy of
the honor and insufficient for the task. He believed that
he did not have enough courage and skill, and therefore
could not bring the children of Israel out of Egypt. They
were unarmed, undisciplined, and unable to help themselves. Yet, Moses was the fittest of any man living for this
work, eminent in learning, wisdom, experience, valor,
faith, and devotion. Yet he asked, Who am I? Sometimes
the greatest leaders feel the least qualified.

Moses said to the LORD, "O Lord, I have never been
eloquent, neither in the past nor since you have spoken to your servant. I am slow of speech and
tongue."

The LORD said to him, "Who gave man his
mouth? Who makes him deaf or mute? Who gives

him sight or makes him blind? Is it not I, the LORD?

"Now go; I will help you speak and will teach you what to say."

EXODUS 4:10-12 NIV

God responded to Moses' objections with the promise of His presence. "And God said, 'I will be with you,'" and that was enough. Those who are weak in themselves can do wonders if they are strong in the Lord and in the power of His might. Those who are most timid may be most confident in God. His presence makes the greatest difficulties dwindle to nothing.

SECRET TO SUCCESSFUL LEADERSHIP

When Moses was in exile, he dealt with his own limitations at the deepest level, questioning who he was and what he was to be. He had had no religious upbringing or experience with God. He had given little or no thought to God, and he didn't know how to have a relationship with God. But the magnitude of what Moses did was unprecedented and incredible. He led over six hundred thousand Hebrews on foot through numerous countries for forty years. And in the process Moses became a man of deep devotion to God.

Moses would get the direction he needed to lead his "corporation" of over six hundred thousand people from his devotional life. Out of the time he spent with Jehovah, he received the laws and moral codes for the "company." Moses sought the presence of God in worship for the good of the nation. His ability to lead and his strength came from his spiritual life. His relationship with God was part of his business and not a separate part of his life.

FOLLOWING THE CLOUD

Moses shows us the key to being great leaders: letting God lead. Moses was a man in control but became dependent on the Lord. He led by following. He did not move until God moved. When the cloud of God's presence moved, then Moses would follow, leading Israel in the same direction. He was responsive to the Lord.

Moses became a good follower because he had the heart of a worshiper. Other men try to be great leaders by getting God to follow them. "Here are my plans, God. Would you please bless them?" they pray. But like Moses, great leaders get involved in doing "God's thing" instead of doing their own thing.

We can learn a lesson in priorities from Moses, too. Moses didn't care to be a leader of over six hundred thousand people. He put God first. He would rather follow God than lead a nation. In the same way, we must put *God's* leadership first. Then we will be great leaders.

Worshiping the Lord and intently seeking His face will give us a spiritual connection with the Lord. This involves prayer, reading the Bible, and singing to the Lord. This kind of lifestyle will give us an advantage as leaders. Our values and attitudes will create the kind of man our fellow workers want to follow and our customers can count on.

We can see this principle of leading by following again in the Book of Revelation. The twenty-four leaders in heaven had dominion and authority but repeatedly set their faces toward the throne. They were followers of a greater authority.

> Surrounding the throne were twenty-four other thrones, and seated on them were twenty-four elders. They were dressed in white and had crowns of gold on their heads.
>
> REVELATION 4:4, NIV

These men are intimates of God. Their proximity to the throne signifies their relationship with God. Their crowns denote their authority and honor. These are men who have obtained stature and position. They are representatives of people, significant leaders. You could easily conclude that the highest place of authority to which any human could ever rise is to the position of one of the twenty-four elders that surround the throne of God. But look at the nature and character of their position:

> They lay their crowns before the throne and say: "You are worthy, our Lord and God, to receive glory and honor and power, for you created all things, and by your will they were created and have their being."
>
> REVELATION 4:10-11, NIV

The twenty-four elders, who sit on their thrones before God, fell on their faces and worshiped God, saying, "We give Thee thanks, O Lord God, the Almighty, who art and who was, because Thou hast taken Thy great power and hast begun to reign."

REVELATION 11:16-17, KJV

We do not have to wait until eternity to establish an intimate relationship with God. We can put Him first in whatever we are doing today. How do we become great leaders? By following God. We seek to do His thing, rather than our own, and we can learn to be responsive to His leading. In this way, we become the sort of men that others will want to follow.

GOD'S HAMMER

Many men have a heart to get close to God, but they are not sure they know how. Like Moses, they see the fire at the top of the mountain, but they do not know how to get there. There is only one way we can know God: we have to climb the mountain. Moses had a strong desire to know God and took deliberate action. It takes effort to seek the Lord in worship.

A few years ago a friend of mine was feeling spiritually dead. He couldn't figure out what was wrong. God showed him that, though he still believed in the general providence of God, he no longer believed in God's specific providence. He could see God's hand in the big things in life, but it was difficult for him to see the Lord leading in the little things. So he had given up seeking guidance from God every day for the small, routine decisions.

This man had taken up what I call a "trial mentality." Every difficulty became a great trial. He saw himself as forever going through the wilderness. Joy, happiness, and praise turned into grumbling and complaining. He began to feel very distant from God. He was getting to the place where he made decisions and conducted his business by simply asking God to bless it rather than seeking God for guidance. He had quit seeking God routinely.

Many Christians believe in the general providence of God and, therefore, pray only when the big decisions in life are looming. They do not pray about the many routine things that happen each day. Other Christians believe in the specific providence of the Lord. They trust in God to lead them in every decision, large and small. This is how we should live every day. We can live in such close communion with God that we look for God to direct us daily. We continually seek Him and thank Him for everything that happens.

Spiritual erosion results when we do not maintain our daily worship life. Our belief and sense in His guiding dissipates, and we end up trudging through life by our own compass and not following the Lord. We initiate things without asking Him, and when they do not work out, we blame everyone but ourselves. Moses kept focused on God and did not let himself wander away. As a result, his leadership was prophetic. He listened to what the Lord told him and then repeated it to those he was leading.

Moses did not become a great follower of God overnight. This corporate executive had been groomed for his success by humility and brokenness. Before God called him, Moses had been used to making all the decisions, and he had climbed almost to the top of the political ladder. Yet he found himself in the middle of the desert, disgraced and a fugitive. Sometimes the situations or circumstances in which we find ourselves are the hammers God uses to forge us into good leaders—if we are willing to follow and be changed.

SEEKING HIS FACE

Today we have the Bible that tells us about the character of God and the principles of His kingdom. In Moses' day there was no written revelation of God. Moses came to know this "God of the Hebrews" by looking for him in the experiences of life. He welcomed every opportunity to learn and interact with God. Moses' passion for God was deep. He often sought God's presence and found himself in an intimate place with God.

No prophet has risen in Israel like Moses, whom the LORD knew face to face, who did all those miraculous signs and wonders the LORD sent him to do in Egypt—to Pharaoh and to all his officials and to his whole land. For no one has ever shown the mighty power or performed the awesome deeds that Moses did in the sight of all Israel.

DEUTERONOMY 34:10-12, NIV

I am most intrigued by the many times and the different ways that the power of God's presence was experienced by Moses. A passage from Exodus 33 reveals his friendship with Yahweh:

> Now Moses used to take a tent and pitch it *outside the camp some distance away,* calling it the *"tent of meeting."* Anyone inquiring of the LORD would go to the tent of meeting outside the camp. And whenever Moses went out to the tent, all the people rose and stood at the entrances to their tents, watching Moses until he entered the tent. As Moses went into the tent, the pillar of cloud would come down and stay at the entrance, while the LORD spoke with Moses. Whenever the people saw the pillar of cloud standing at the entrance to the tent, they *all stood and worshiped,* each at the entrance to his tent. The LORD would *speak to Moses face to face, as a man speaks with his friend.* Then Moses would return to the camp, but his young aide Joshua son of Nun did not leave the tent.
>
> EXODUS 33:7-11, NIV (emphasis mine)

I can just see Moses picking up his tent stakes and skin coverings and carrying them outside of the camp. He wanted to get away from the hustle and bustle of daily life. He retreated to be with the Lord. Moses had a hunger for God. It was a matter of priority with him to worship God and inquire of His presence.

Moses didn't accidentally stumble into intimacy with

God; he made a conscious decision to meet with God. He pulled up his tent stakes, gathered his animal skin tent and carried it outside his busy environment so that he could be close to his Lord.

When Moses saw the column of cloud descending over the tent it meant the Lord wanted to speak to him. Moses would go into the tent, and God would speak to him words no other man could hear. When Moses was on Mount Sinai God spoke and gave him the Ten Commandments. The Lord was communicating clearly and distinctly as Moses remained in the presence of God for forty days and nights. When he descended the mountain Moses' face glowed with the residual glory of God.

Moses was an inspiration and example to the rest of the men. They would watch when he went into the presence of God and communed with Him. Today this kind of intimate worship is not only for church leaders but for all of us. We all can come into the presence of the Lord and worship Him "face to face."

How many men today can say that they know God face to face? They are the men who climb the mountain daily to seek Him. They have learned to respond to God and to follow His leading. Like Moses, men who are devoted to God reflect a residue of the presence of God in their lives—in the way they conduct their business, relate to their family, and give directions to their subordinates. They can be distinguished by their attitudes and the way they interact with others. They have learned to respond to God's leading and in turn have become the kind of men others want to follow.

■ ■ ■ ■ ■

TEN

A Man with a Mission

John had an appetite for success. He could smell a good deal. Making money was in his blood and the passion of his life. John would lie awake at night and dream of better deals and creative ways to multiply his personal and business cash reserves.

John was pleased with his achievements. He'd been involved in starting several businesses that grossed over a million a year. He negotiated large corporate acquisitions that brought him significant respect in the business world. John made sure that everyone he met sooner or later became aware of what he had done. He wanted to be a contender for the most successful businessman of the year—every year.

John was good at what he did. He could sell more units than anyone else in the company. At the end of the day John wanted to feel that he had accomplished something significant. So he would work until he made some great achievement or just ran out of hours in the day.

Carol, John's wife, didn't see much of her husband. There was no normal routine in their home. Carol gave up planning meals with the whole family. She couldn't depend on her husband being home at any certain time.

The first ten years were okay, but after that, Carol began to feel lonely. She tried to reach out for friends who could encourage and strengthen her. Life had become a bore with the drudgery of her own routine and no husband with whom to share her deepest feelings and frustrations. Carol had lost most of her romantic feelings for John long ago. Sex had become an obligation. Carol began to seriously wonder, *Is this all there will ever be to my life?* She longed for John to take interest in her. She wanted to go on dates, laugh, and just have some fun.

The children didn't expect to see their father until the weekend—that is, if he didn't go out of town. John's sons played their baseball games without their dad's input or presence. Carol and the children decided on what their family activities would be, and she shuttled them to all their events. John seemed always to be somewhere else conquering another deal. Even if he was with the family, his mind was somewhere else.

"I want to be the best!" John would always say. He wasn't afraid of the challenges of new conflicts. "I'll make it happen!" he would often brag. "I'll do it if it kills me!" John was consumed to achieve.

The problem was that his drive and mission indeed were killing him, but he couldn't see it. He'd get so wound up during the day that he couldn't sleep at night. John needed two or three drinks to calm down at the end of the day. His dependency on alcohol began to grow. He made sure there were always several bottles in the office.

John would get angry and raise his voice when he had too much to drink. His family and friends, those closest to him, were the ones that suffered from his mood swings. John was destroying his life.

John's family was slowly deteriorating. His eldest son was experimenting with drugs because of the friends he had made in his father's absence. Carol told her son to find other friends, but the children seldom honored their mother's wishes. John had never enforced any discipline in the home. Consequently, the children did what they wanted.

"I'll make it if it kills me!" John continued to say. It became a self-fulfilling prophecy. His drive to climb the corporate ladder was destroying his whole world. Physically, emotionally, spiritually, and mentally, everyone in his family was suffering. They had all the money they needed, but money didn't mean that much anymore. They were all hurting because of their father's self-centered ambitions.

DRIVEN TO SUCCEED

Some men can never find time to worship because they are driven to do so many things. They may be visionaries propelled to reach new plateaus in their careers. To them these agendas are of such importance that worshiping the Lord gets left to the end of the day. By then there is no time and no energy left. I want to point out several characteristics of men who are compulsively driven.

1. Driven men are satisfied only with achievement.
From early childhood we are taught that our value as a
person is based on our accomplishments. Men tend to see
life only in terms of results. There is little appreciation for
the process leading toward the accomplishment. Often we
view worship in the same way. In our eyes worship must
have a result or benefit. We justify not worshiping the
Lord because we don't see any results out of the time
invested. We have little appreciation for the process of
worship—the interaction, the relationship, or the communication.

**2. Driven men are often task-oriented and preoccu-
pied with the symbols of accomplishment.** Status, titles,
and the symbols of importance are the focus of a man's
attention. Our own notoriety is our concern. This attitude
distracts us from worship. If a phone rings when a driven
man is trying to pray, he can never just leave it to the
answering machine. The call gives him a feeling of importance or prestige and appeals to his task orientation. Who,
though, is more important than the One he was talking to
before the phone rang?

**3. Driven men tend to have less concern for integrity
and are more vulnerable to compromise.** We often are
so preoccupied with success and achievement that we have
little time to stop and listen to the Lord in worship.
Consequently, our inner life is weakened. Our integrity
breaks down when we don't have time to spend with the
Lord. Our connection with Him becomes more distant.

We compromise, here a little and there a little, and before you know it there are major problems. It all happens because we let the urgent take priority over the important. Compromised morals and values gradually occur. We must keep worship our highest priority.

4. Men who are driven often lack developed people skills. "People skills" are usually undeveloped in driven men. Projects are more important to them than people. Men like this rarely take notice of people around them unless those people are necessary to accomplish their objectives. Their "to do" list pulls them to run into the day without communing with the Lord. Likewise, if they get around to worship at all, it too becomes an objective to be fulfilled rather than a relationship to be enjoyed.

CONSUMED WITH THE WRONG MISSION

Saul was a type "A" personality. Saul possessed a zealous ambition that drove him to want to be the best and accomplish the most.

Born in Tarsus (modern-day Turkey) in A.D. 6, Saul lived a hard life for about fifty-eight years. He grew up in a Greek cultural center but was sent off to Jerusalem for his schooling. There he studied the Jewish Scriptures and religious law under a well-respected and renowned rabbi, Gamaliel, also known as "the Elder" (Acts 22:3). Gamaliel was a member of the Sanhedrin, a Jewish ruling council.

Saul was extreme in everything he did. He was a part of

the strictest sect of the Jews—the Pharisees (Acts 26:5). He was a devoted Jew and proud of his heritage and traditions. He had no patience with the members of the Messianic sect called "The Way," who followed the teaching of the recently executed Jesus. This sect threatened all that he was and passionately stood for, and so Saul joined wholeheartedly in the efforts to eradicate them.

At a meeting of the Sanhedrin, Stephen, a follower of "The Way," was indicting the Jews for their rejection of God's messenger and their unbelief in Jesus Christ. The members of the Sanhedrin were enraged and gnashed their teeth at Stephen. "But Stephen, full of the Holy Spirit, looked up to heaven and saw the glory of God, and Jesus standing at the right hand of God. 'Look,' he said, 'I see heaven open and the Son of Man standing at the right hand of God.'" They rushed upon him, dragged him outside the city and stoned him.

> Meanwhile, the witnesses laid their clothes at the feet of a young man named Saul. While they were stoning him, Stephen prayed, "Lord Jesus, receive my spirit." Then he fell on his knees and cried out, "Lord, do not hold this sin against them." When he had said this, he fell asleep.
>
> ACTS 7:55-60, NIV

Saul was present at Stephen's stoning. In fact, Scripture says that Saul heartily approved of putting Stephen to death (Acts 8:1). He may have known Stephen well. They could have gone to the same synagogue. But Saul reacted with rage toward his peers who had become the followers of the crucified criminal. The gospel was making inroads into the synagogue, and Saul was determined to stop it. It did not bother him that in his zeal he was helping to murder others. "Saul began to destroy the church. Going from house to house, he dragged off men and women and put them in prison" (Acts 8:3, NIV).

Saul was a highly motivated man—a man on a mission. In his own words he was a "Hebrew of the Hebrews" and a "Pharisee of Pharisees" (Phil 3:5). When he became a persecutor of the church, he did it with a passion. He was committed to his goal of finding every Christian in the country. His mission to destroy or incarcerate each follower of Christ consumed him.

Saul was still breathing out murderous threats against the Lord's disciples. He went to the high priest and asked him for letters to the synagogues in Damascus, so that if he found any there who belonged to the Way, whether men or women, he might take them as prisoners to Jerusalem.

ACTS 9:1-2, NIV

On the way to achieving his goals, the Creator of heaven and earth arrested him.

As he neared Damascus on his journey, suddenly a light from heaven flashed around him. He fell to the ground and heard a voice say to him, "Saul, Saul, why do you persecute me?" "Who are you, Lord?"

Saul asked. "I am Jesus, whom you are persecuting," he replied. "Now get up and go into the city, and you will be told what you must do."

The men traveling with Saul stood there speechless; they heard the sound but did not see anyone. Saul got up from the ground, but when he opened his eyes he could see nothing. So they led him by the hand into Damascus.

ACTS 9:3-8, NIV

When Saul arrived in Damascus, Ananias prayed for him, and something like scales fell from his eyes. He was physically healed as well as filled with the Holy Spirit. At that moment Saul became a follower of Christ. He was convinced that Jesus was alive and was calling him to a special mission. His religious beliefs changed drastically. His goals and mission changed. He began to proclaim Jesus, the one whom he formerly persecuted. Once the devout Pharisee, Saul accepted as his life's mission the task of taking the gospel to the Gentiles. And he took on a new Greek name, Paul.

GIVING IT ALL AWAY

Paul's type "A" personality was now focused on a new mission—reaching the Gentiles with the gospel. To accomplish this goal he would have to cross political, cultural, and religious barriers. He was so bold and effective at his mission that his former colleagues tried to murder him on at least two occasions. He stirred up entire cities against him, winning thousands of converts in the process. He became the Christian church's greatest missionary.

Driven to work hard because of his personality, Paul was relentless in pursuing his goals. Paul was compelled to reach the Gentiles, that is, the rest of the entire non-Jewish world. That was a big vision.

> For thus the Lord has commanded us, "I have placed you as a light for the Gentiles, that you should bring salvation to the *end of the earth*."
> ACTS 13:47, NASB (emphasis mine)

This ambition caused him to spend 25 percent of his life in prison. He continued in his cause undaunted by floggings, death threats, murder attempts, imprisonment, and shipwrecks.

The key to Paul's success as a missionary was that he was able to give his ambitions and his dreams to God. He saw his ministry as something to be offered up as an act of worship. He wrote to the church in Rome that he was "a minister of Christ Jesus to the Gentiles, ministering as a priest the gospel of God, that my offering of the Gentiles might become acceptable, sanctified by the Holy Spirit" (Rm 15:16, NASB).

Paul's job was an extension of his worship life, and the profits and proceeds became sacrifices to God. Whatever Paul did he did it as "unto" the Lord. Paul viewed his job as a grace entrusted to him. "But by the grace of God I am what I am, and his grace to me was not without effect. No, I worked harder than all of them—yet not I, but the grace of God that was with me" (1 Cor 15:10, NIV). Paul labored not in his own efforts but by the grace of God working through him.

Our mission in life is given to us by God as a stewardship. We do not have to be in the ministry for our work to be worship to God. Writing contracts and selling inventory can be an act of worship. "Whatever you do, whether in word or deed, do it all in the name of the Lord Jesus, giving thanks to God the Father through him" (Col 3:17, NIV).

Sometimes it is difficult for men to ask God for help or to give our goals and business life to God. But we should not be discouraged; we are not alone. Sometimes difficulties like these are a signal that God wants us to call out to Him. Have we become too self-reliant, so confident in our own abilities and resources that we have forgotten our worship life? God may bring us to the end of ourselves so we will cry out to Him.

It is interesting that both Moses and Paul, very qualified and successful men, both had to encounter God's presence to find their destiny. They were both arrested by the manifest presence of God that shook their lives. He gave them each a new mission that represented a 180 degree course correction. Moses went back to his boss and challenged him to let the Hebrews go. Paul promoted the gospel instead of persecuting the church. Both men had dramatic turnarounds in their lives because of a worship encounter with God.

THE SECRET TO ACHIEVING GREAT THINGS

It is at the height of one's drivenness, as in the case of Paul, and in the depths of one's mistakes, as with Moses, that God wants to reveal Himself to us. Paul was a driven man. Moses was a broken man. Both had training and experience in leading, yet they learned to follow the Great Leader. Men who learn to tap into God's grace and power accomplish great things. Paul boasted about his abilities in this way:

> But he said to me, "My grace is sufficient for you, for my power is made perfect in weakness." Therefore I will boast all the more gladly about my weaknesses, so that Christ's power may rest on me. That is why, for Christ's sake, I delight in weaknesses, in insults, in hardships, in persecutions, in difficulties. For when I am weak, then I am strong.
>
> 2 CORINTHIANS 12:9-10, NIV

Grace is in the person of the Holy Spirit, Who is our Helper. It is His presence that goes with us when we do our business, and it is His presence we find when we worship. Both our drivenness and our brokenness can become "gates to grace." Our weaknesses are opportunities for God to be really strong in us.

Let us not forget that we can do no thing apart from God. He is the vine and we are the branches. If we remain in Him through regular intimate worship, we will bear fruit. No branch can bear fruit alone. It must stay in the vine. If we dwell in Him, and He remains in us, then we will bear much fruit (see John 15).

■ ■ ■ ■ ■

ELEVEN

A Man Under Stress

David was the youngest of his seven brothers. Some would have called him the runt of the litter. Being the youngest, he was not asked to do large, significant tasks. Often he was asked to do the menial, like take care of the sheep. But his low standing was an opportunity to find God. There wasn't much to do in the field with the sheep except keep a peripheral view on what was going on around them. It afforded David many chances to sing.

David often took his harp with him and sang about his faith in God. Many times he would sing "to" God. His work and worship were mixed together in a glorious harmony. His musical abilities grew as well as his relationship with his God. David became strong in his inner world because of his strong devotional life.

David's habit of intimate worship would one day equip him to deal with large amounts of stress. His relationship with God is what kept him through betrayal, adultery, murder, and the responsibilities of running a kingdom. All of these situations carried with them large doses of stress and tension. Yet David maintained his devotional life through strains in his relationships and the stress of his royal business.

On the other hand, Saul, who, like David, reigned as king over Israel for thirty-two years, had some of the same stressful situations and temptations, but he had not developed his devotional worship life with God. Although God had touched Saul's heart in his early years, causing him to prophesy with the prophets (see 1 Samuel 10:10-11), Saul disobeyed God and followed his own way. He justified himself rather than confessing his sin before God. He did not devote himself to the habit of worship and prayer.

Both kings, David and Saul, had power and privilege. Both were anointed by Samuel. But both made serious mistakes during their lives. Each experienced times of much depression and even felt that God had abandoned him. Yet, they handled the situations very differently.

When David felt the stress, he would pray to God in song. It helped him deal with difficulties effectively.

Hear my prayer, O LORD; let my cry for help come to you. Do not hide your face from me when I am in distress. Turn your ear to me; when I call, answer me quickly.

PSALMS 102:1-2, NIV

David would pour out his lament to God.

All day long my enemies taunt me; those who rail against me use my name as a curse. For I eat ashes as my food and mingle my drink with tears.

PSALMS 102:8-9, NIV

David was honest with God. He knew that the Lord would be his source of deliverance in every situation.

> But you, O LORD, sit enthroned forever; your renown endures through all generations. You will arise and have compassion on Zion, for it is time to show favor to her; the appointed time has come.
>
> PSALMS 102:12-13, NIV

In song David would pour out his complaint to God and then declare the provision of God. He sung of his own deliverance. When we worship we are inspired by the presence of God. Answers come to our questions when we worship. Faith, courage, and hope arise when we worship because of the inspiring presence of God.

When Saul was distressed he didn't call out to God. He would call for David, the worshiping musician of his court. He did not call out to God for himself.

> Saul's attendants said to him, "See, an evil spirit from God is tormenting you. Let our lord command his servants here to search for someone who can play the harp. He will play when the evil spirit from God comes upon you, and you will feel better."
>
> 1 SAMUEL 16:15-16, NIV

In Saul's agony there was no presence of God in his life to comfort and inspire him. He had no relationship with the Lord. He had to depend on the worship of another.

Whenever the evil spirit from God came to Saul, David would take the harp and play it with his hand; and Saul would be refreshed and be well, and the evil spirit would depart from him.

1 SAMUEL 16:23, NASB

There was no inner spiritual life that sustained Saul. He did not have enough inner glow to spark a song of his own. He could only listen to David's. Saul had to be spiritually fed from the outside because there was no spiritual strength that came from within.

Men today rely on their pastors' faith to encourage them on Sunday morning if, that is, they can make it to the service with all the pressures they have. Some are thankful for their wives' worship to bring the presence of God into their homes and give direction.

It is a sad state to be dependent on another person's devotional life to sustain us. Many of us are sustained by external things. Today we have access to innumerable opportunities to stimulate our souls from without. When those things change or we get "unplugged" from them, there is no source from within to bring life and strength. We each need to find God for ourselves. God must be our individual and personal source of all that we need. That connection with God comes from a life of devotion in worship.

David said, "All my springs of joy are in you" (Ps 87:7, NASB). Whether he was sad or happy, depressed or triumphant, sick or well, offended or forgiving, stressed or at peace, David would focus on his spiritual source of life—the worship of God.

Men who are weak in their worship lives will decline in their virtue and succumb to the pressures of the world around them when they are under pressure. It is when we lose our job or business that we are tempted to compromise. Catastrophic events in our lives sometime force men to lose their integrity and to do the wrong things. Under stress our true character is revealed.

Life will continually drain our strength and peace. These can only be restored and recharged in the presence of the "I Am." Whether we are spiritual leaders or business leaders, we must stay tapped into the source of our spiritual life.

"FAIR WEATHER" WORSHIP

When we get under pressure the first thing to go is our prayer and worship life. Why is that? Could it be because our devotional life doesn't consist of worship, only thanksgiving? We can be thankful when everything is going well. Then it is easy to worship. But that is only "fair weather" worship.

Praise and worship should be the most consistent part of our devotional life, but it should have nothing to do with how well things are going for us. Neither is it related to the way we feel. It is based on God and not our situations.

Are we like Saul or David? When things didn't go well for Saul his worship life fell apart. When things fell apart for David it drove him to God. Even in distress David ran to God and poured out his heart.

"Seven times a day I praise you for your righteous laws" (Ps 119:164, NIV), a psalmist sang. Morning, noon, and night we can praise Him even when things are rough. Praise and worship is the foundation of our devotional lives.

David said, "One thing I have asked from the LORD, that I shall seek: that I may dwell in the house of the LORD all the days of my life, to behold the beauty of the LORD, and to meditate in his temple." His desire was to be in God's presence and commune with the Lord. There he knew he was safe and secure.

> For in the day of trouble he will conceal me in his tabernacle; in the secret place of his tent he will hide me; he will lift me up on a rock. And now my head will be lifted up above my enemies around me; and I will offer in his tent sacrifices with shouts of joy; I will sing, yes, I will sing praises to the LORD.
>
> PSALMS 27:4-6, NASB

In the secret place of God's presence David was elevated above his enemies. It is amazing the longitudes and latitudes we can see from the heights of God's presence in worship. There David could sing and shout for joy, and so can we.

Worship is not the "sound of music" but the "sound of the heart." The integrity of worship is determined by the integrity of the heart. David had developed a mature heart of worship and God blessed him.

God is interested in our heart too. We are to love Him with all our heart, not only all our talent, because the heart is His concern. "How blessed are those who observe his testimonies, who seek him with *all their heart*" (Ps 119:2, NASB, emphasis mine).

When the Lord sees us He does not see our good looks or our abilities. He sees our heart. Yet we spend so much time on fixing the outward. The story of how David was chosen tells us something about what God looks for in a man.

When they arrived, Samuel saw Eliab and thought, "Surely the LORD's anointed stands here before the LORD." But the LORD said to Samuel, "Do not consider his appearance or his height, for I have rejected him. The LORD does not look at the things man looks at. Man looks at the outward appearance, but the LORD looks at the heart."

Then Jesse called Abinadab and had him pass in front of Samuel. But Samuel said, "The LORD has not chosen this one either." Jesse then had Shammah pass by, but Samuel said, "Nor has the LORD chosen this one." Jesse had seven of his sons pass before Samuel, but Samuel said to him, "The LORD has not chosen these." So he asked Jesse, "Are these all the sons you have?" "There is still the youngest," Jesse answered, "but he is tending the sheep." Samuel said, "Send for him; we will not sit down until he arrives."

So he sent and had him brought in. He was ruddy, with a fine appearance and handsome features. Then

the LORD said, "Rise and anoint him; he is the one."
So Samuel took the horn of oil and anointed him in
the presence of his brothers, and from that day on
the Spirit of the LORD came upon David in power.
Samuel then went to Ramah.

1 SAMUEL 16:6-13, NIV

David was chosen by the Lord because of his heart. His
priorities were most like God's priorities. Have you ever
wondered how that happened? Very simple—they spent
time together early in David's life, and God shaped
David's heart.

There have been times in my life when I have drunk
from someone else's spiritual reservoirs—someone who
had a deep flow of the presence of God. I longed to be
like them. Just talking with them was fulfilling and satisfy-
ing to my spirit and their lives convicted me of my shal-
lowness. How I wanted to walk with God as they did. But
I know there is no shortcut to being filled up with God's
presence and comfort. I know that to tap into God's life
and strength, we must regularly experience His presence
in worship—in singing, praising, and thanksgiving. And
no one else can do that for us—we must do it for ourselves.

■ ■ ■ ■ ■

TWELVE

A Man with Vision

The voice came out of nowhere and thundered with ominous power. "Leave your country, your people and your father's household and go to the land I will show you" (Gn 12:1, NIV). A supernatural presence surrounded Abram. "I will make you into a great nation and I will bless you; I will make your name great, and you will be a blessing" (Gn 12:2, NIV).

Abram had no choice but to believe what he heard. The confirming power of the divine presence validated the words he heard. Abram's family had always worshiped idols in southern Babylon, but those gods had never spoken to him.

Abram was assured by the words "I will make you a great nation" because his wife had long been barren. Children were very important to a man in that culture, particularly to Abram. His name meant "exalted father."

God's promise that Abram would one day be a father was a trial of faith to Abram. Sarai could not have children, and so what Abram had heard from God was impossible from a human standpoint. But Abram felt sure that God could make the promise good. God's presence was so real, the promise had to be real, too.

"I will bless those who bless you, and whoever curses you I will curse; and all peoples on earth will be blessed through you" (Gn 12:3, NIV). Abram fell to the ground overwhelmed by the force of the presence of God and the magnitude of what He was saying.

"There was no mistaking what I heard from this divine One!" Abram must have assured his wife. "We must obey what He has said." Abram and his family began packing, not knowing where they were going. They were about to follow a God they did not know.

Abram's destiny was about to unfold. The entire direction of his life was to dramatically turn around. He would exchange the gods he had long worshiped for another that he did not know or understand. He would move to a foreign country and start over. The dynamics of the new direction in his life would be so tremendous that his name would change to Abraham, the father of multitudes. He would become the first great patriarch of ancient Israel and a primary role model of faith for all of Christianity.

Those who walk with God must trust Him. We must forsake things that are seen for things that are not seen. Like Abram, men today are called by God to lands they have not seen. We must keep our eyes on Him, and we must move forward with vision.

GIVING UP THE VISION

At the age of one hundred years, Abraham saw his dream come to pass. God gave him a son. His name was Isaac. The promise was fulfilled. Isaac was Abraham's pride and joy. Not only was Abraham a father, but there was a possibility now that the promise of his being a father of a nation could come true. Now things started to make sense. Abram could now see how God was going to do what He said. Everything started to look up.

One day God told Abraham to take Isaac and offer him as a sacrifice of worship (see Genesis 22:1-19). It was as if God was saying, "Let your vision die." Abraham did not argue with God. He promptly took Isaac to Mount Moriah according to God's instructions and, after three days of travel, prepared to kill his only son. Abraham's faith in God was so great that he was willing to sacrifice what must have appeared to be the only source of fulfillment for his vision.

Leaving the servants behind, Abraham and his son went up Mount Moriah with the fire, wood, and a knife. When they reached the place, Abraham built an altar and laid out wood. He bound his son and placed him on the wood. He lifted his knife into the air, ready to kill Isaac, his son of promise. Abraham did not hesitate hoping for a way out. His confident reliance was on God. Abraham was willing to sacrifice his dreams and vision in obedience to God.

Suddenly there was a voice from heaven. "Abraham, Abraham."

Abraham replied, "I'm here."

"Do not harm your son! I now know that you fear God because you will not keep your son from me, not even your only son," God thundered.

At that time Abraham saw a ram caught in a bush and killed it, instead of his son, as a sacrifice to God. God did not tell Abraham that he was to use the ram to sacrifice instead of his son. It was in Abraham's heart to worship God out of obedience. Then God said:

> "I swear by myself," declares the LORD, "that because you have done this and have not withheld your son, your only son, I will surely bless you and make your descendants as numerous as the stars in the sky and as the sand on the seashore. Your descendants will take possession of the cities of their enemies, and through your offspring all nations on earth will be blessed, because you have obeyed me."
>
> GENESIS 22:16-18, NIV

From this one man, whom God considered faithful and who considered God faithful, came descendants as numerous as the stars in the sky and as countless as the sand on the seashore. Abraham became known as the "Father of Faith" as a result. He is the "father of us all" (Rom 4:16, Gal 3:7, NIV). He was also called the "friend of God" (Jas 2:23).

"[Abram] believed the LORD, and he credited it to him as righteousness" (Gn 15:6, NIV). Abraham did not waver in unbelief but knew that God could do what He promised He would do. By faith Abraham pursued the vision that God gave him.

Abraham was a man of great devotion and worship. At many strategic points in his life he would build altars to worship God. From this man, thanksgiving and sacrifice flowed freely. Not only did Abraham build the altar of stones and offer animal sacrifices on the burning wood, but he would call on the name of the Lord. That means he would cry out to God in an attempt to draw near to Him. It was a process of seeking the Lord. These stone altars were memorials to what God had done in his life. They were times to remember how the Lord spoke to him and how God revealed Himself. At these altars Abraham would take his children and recount the moments of encounter with God.

Abraham had a lifestyle of seeking the Lord in worship. Without a tutor or any model to follow, Abraham did what his heart told him and discovered worship through the offering of sacrifice at these altars. The word "altar" in Hebrew means a place of slaughter or sacrifice. Abraham's worship consisted of offering sacrifice to atone for sin and restore fellowship with God.

Abraham's worship can be a model for us. When we get off track spiritually, we are to go back to the last altar we built in our spiritual lives and remember what happened there. What did God say at that time? This is the beginning of returning to a deeper relationship with God. If we are cold, dark, and desperate for the Lord, it helps to recall the last place we found Him. Can we get back to that and visit with God about where we are now? There we can simply ask Him for help.

Abraham's heart was found by God to be faithful and pure, the character of a man who regularly worships. Despite impossible odds, Abraham had faith in the promises of God, and he never gave up the vision of his dreams. He maintained his close relationship with God because he was a worshiper. Perhaps that is how his faith could be sustained so long in the face of mocking circumstances.

Whether we are corporate executives, small business owners, blue collar workers, ministers, accountants, or musicians there is a call on our lives as men to be real and to worship. You can be more of a man than you realize. You can be spiritual and caring, responsible and effective. I pray that you will be. If you want to grow as a man, pray this prayer with me.

Heavenly Father, I praise You for Your greatness and Your goodness. With You all things are possible. You can help me become a real man—the man You want me to be—caring, understanding, loving, spiritual, responsible, and serving.

I pray for the best for my wife and children. I commit my life and resources for their spiritual growth. May I be the father and husband they need. Help me, Lord, give them my best.

Give me the ability and insight to grow my inner world. Help me groom the garden of my heart, killing the weeds that steal and kill my spiritual life. May the fruit of the kingdom of God be seen in my heart and evidenced in my attitudes and actions. Make me more like Christ.

Give me a new passion for Your Word and for Your presence, committing myself to do anything necessary to find You in my busy schedule. May I be uncomfortable when I miss my time with You. Make me the worshiper You desire—a real man.

In Jesus' Name. Amen.

■ ■ ■ ■ ■

Practical Helps to Worship

Almost every Christian struggles with personality weaknesses, habitual tendencies, dysfunctional characteristics, and a wide variety of other "flesh hassles." Often as leaders we believe that there isn't anyone we can talk to about our weaknesses and the wars we fight in our private worlds. All of us have to "work out" and "walk out" our salvation day to day by waging war with the weakness that affects our inner man.

How can we help each other in the struggles we face and thereby improve our worship?

The private world of our hearts is the incubator of our individual worship. Our hearts determine the integrity of our worship. We want to increase that quality of worship by overcoming the darkness in our hearts. All of us have a desire to have a heart that pleases the Lord.

"*May the words* of my mouth and the *meditation of my heart* be *pleasing* in your sight, O LORD, my Rock and my Redeemer" (Ps 19:14, NIV, emphasis mine). The author of this prophetic song, Psalm 19, knows where the willful sins come from and where they must be dealt with—in the heart.

To deal with these secret and not-so-secret weaknesses

we must bring light into our private world. This can be done by confessing our private faults to someone we trust.

> This then is the message which we have heard of him, and declare unto you, that God is light, and in him is no darkness at all. If we say that we have fellowship with him, and walk in darkness, we lie, and do not tell the truth: But if we *walk in the light,* as he is in the light, we have *fellowship one with another,* and the blood of Jesus Christ his Son *cleanseth us from all sin.* If we say that we have no sin, we deceive ourselves, and the truth is not in us.
>
> 1 JOHN 1:5-8, KJV, (emphasis mine)

Walking in the light is bringing secret sins and weakness out into the open—into the light. We can do this by confiding in our pastor, our wife, or a close friend. This keeps us from the deception of thinking we can always overcome it ourselves. We keep falling and feeling guilty and think we are unworthy to worship God. As men we condemn ourselves and back out of spiritual activities, thinking subconsciously that we are of no value to the Lord.

Yet the Bible says in the next verse:

> If *we confess our sins,* he is faithful and just to *forgive us our sins,* and to cleanse us from all unrighteousness. If we say that we have not sinned, we make him a liar, and his word is not in us.
>
> 1 JOHN 1:9-10, KJV, (emphasis mine)

There are wicked hearts who plot to sin and have no desire to be exposed. And then there are hearts, like yours and mine, that want to overcome their faults but perhaps have a hard time bringing them into the light. We are afraid of what others will think. Confessing faults to the one we trust (wife, pastor, or friend) puts them in the open so Satan cannot use them against us. He no longer has a foothold in our life.

HOW TO DEAL WITH OUR WEAKNESSES

The first step in overcoming our willful faults is to confess them to the Lord and ask Him for forgiveness. Yes, even if it is the millionth time you have had to do it! For in the same manner in which we "received" salvation, we "work out" our salvation.

If we do confess our sins He is faithful and fair to forgive us those sins and cleanse us from them. The Scripture does not say if we are good enough He will forgive us. It says when we make mistakes and confess them to Him (that is, get them out in the open) He will forgive us. He will forgive us every time. Keep this in mind:

For as the heaven is high above the earth, so great is his mercy toward them that fear him. As far as the east is from the west, so far hath *he removed our transgressions* from us.

PSALMS 103:11-12, KJV, (emphasis mine)

When we sin and ask forgiveness, God removes our sins. They are erased and not remembered anymore. So though you may have failed a thousand times in a certain area of your life, each time you confessed it, you were forgiven. I have more good news: He is not counting! The Lord always forgives and forgets what we have confessed. Psalms 130:4 says, "But with you there is forgiveness; therefore you are feared" (NIV). The Lord says that He will be "merciful to their unrighteousness, and their sins and their iniquities will *I remember no more*" (Heb 8:12, KJV, emphasis mine). He will do the same for us.

I encourage you not to hide your sin but to talk to the Lord about it and confide in someone you trust.

I acknowledged my sin unto thee, and mine iniquity have I not hid. I said, I will confess my transgressions unto the LORD; and thou forgavest the iniquity of my sin. Selah.

PSALMS 32:5, KJV

Another way to see our sins forgiven is to forgive others. If we forgive those that hurt or wound us then God will forgive us. "Judge not, and ye shall not be judged: condemn not, and ye shall not be condemned: forgive, and ye shall be forgiven" (Lk 6:37, KJV). Also, "And forgive us our sins; for we also forgive every one that is indebted to us. And lead us not into temptation; but deliver us from evil" (Lk 11:4, KJV).

CAN ANOTHER MAN CONFIDE IN YOU?

If someone comes to you and wants to confess his sins, are you willing to listen to them and trustworthy enough to keep it to yourself? Listen with concern for them, and ask the Lord how you can help them. Pray together, and then check up on them regularly. Put safeguards in their lives to help them overcome their weak areas. Be faithful to them.

Blessed is he whose transgressions are forgiven, whose *sins are covered.* Blessed is the man whose sin the LORD does not count against him and in whose *spirit is no deceit.*

PSALMS 32:1-2, NIV, (emphasis mine)

HECTIC OR HOLY?

Are you under stress? Are you running around at a hectic pace? Are your nerves frayed and your emotional reserves low? Do you snap at your children? Do you bark at your wife? Could you be described as more hectic than holy? To be holy, we have to set ourselves apart with God on a regular basis. When was the last time you consistently set yourself apart to worship God?

If your life is getting out of hand, below are some practical and thought-provoking questions to ask yourself. Sit down (with your wife, if you are married) and consider:

1. Which things are most important to you and your family?
2. Which things are important but not essential?
3. Which things are helpful but not necessary?
4. Which things are of minor significance?

Now eliminate everything in categories three and four. By doing this, you can cut out a lot of unnecessary activity and not seriously affect your productivity. Another experiment? Devote an entire evening to silence and see what happens, or set aside a time for solitude each day.

THE PLEASURE OF HIS PRESENCE

Recount some of the times that you experienced the Lord's presence. What happened when you encountered God? What were you doing? Where were you at the time?

When he was at the table with them, he took bread, gave thanks, broke it and began to give it to them. Then their *eyes were opened* and they *recognized him*, and he disappeared from their sight. They asked each other, "Were not our hearts burning within us while *he talked with us* on the road and opened *the Scriptures* to us?"

LUKE 24:30-32, NIV, (emphasis mine)

Has your heart burned within you as the Lord spoke to you? Worship will bring you to that place again. Let Him open the Scriptures to you and talk with you. Develop a thirst for God's presence. Prepare to meet with Him.

Notes

ONE
Manhood: A Lost Art?

1. Giora Dilibeto, "Invasion of the Gender Blenders," *People,* April 23, 1984, 97.
2. David Blackenhorn, "Fatherless America," *Christianity Today,* March 6, 1995, 59.
3. As quoted by Steve Farrar in *Point Man* (Portland, Ore.: Multnomah, 1990), 33-34.
4. Ed Cole, *Real Men* (Nashville: Thomas Nelson, 1995), 6.
5. Jim Jones, "He is now in God's hall of fame," *Fort Worth Star-Telegram,* August 20, 1995, C-8.
6. Jones, C-8.
7. Dave Geisler, "Kirk Whalum, Man of Many Passions," *New Man,* August 1995, 23.

THREE
The Inner World of Worship

1. This talk in the General Session of The Worship Institute was given in September, 1995.
2. A.W. Tozer, *Worship: The Missing Jewel of the Evangelical Church* (Camp Hill, Pa.: Christian Publications), 12.

FIVE
The God We Worship

1. Susan Cyre, "Fallout escalates over 'goddess' Sophia worship," *Christianity Today*, April 4, 1994, 74.
2. Cyre.
3. Cyre.
4. Cyre.
5. Cyre.

SIX
Intimacy with God

1. Don McMinn, "General Session," The Worship Institute, Bedford, TX, February 1994.
2. James Robison, "Twenty Lessons Learned While Walking with God," *Charisma & Christian Life Magazine*, August 1995, 60.

3. David Yonggi Cho, "The Best of Charisma," *Charisma & Christian Life Magazine,* August 1995, 54.

EIGHT
Leading Our Families

1. Stephen Covey, Roger and Rebecca Merrill, *First Things First* (New York: Simon & Schuster, 1994), 51, 53.